La Dolce Vita

MITCHELL BEAZLEY

La Dolce Vita

Sweet things from the Italian home kitchen

Ursula Ferrigno

To Sandra Wilson, my husband's aunt, who died suddenly, far too young. She was a truly instinctive cook, and very inspirational. We all miss her so much.

La Dolce Vita
Ursula Ferrigno

First published in Great Britain in 2005 by Mitchell Beazley, an imprint of Octopus Publishing Group Limited, 2–4 Heron Quays, London E14 4JP.
© Octopus Publishing Group Limited 2005
Text © Ursula Ferrigno 2005

A CIP catalogue record for this book is available from the British Library.

ISBN 1 84533 008 0

While all reasonable care has been taken during the preparation of this edition, neither the publisher, editors nor the author can accept responsibility for any consequences arising from the use thereof or from the information contained therein.

Commissioning Editor: Rebecca Spry
Executive Art Editor: Yasia Williams-Leedham
Design: Tim Pattinson
Photography: Francesca Yorke
Home economy: Pippa Cuthbert
Editor: Susan Fleming
Proofreader: Siobhan O'Connor
Production: Seyhan Essen
Index: John Noble

Printed and bound by Toppan Printing Company in China
Typeset in Minion and The Mix

Contents

Introduction

As a nation, the Italians have a very sweet tooth. In fact, the only problem I encountered when gathering together this collection of recipes for puddings, tarts, pastries, ices, cakes, biscuits, sweets and breads was deciding what to leave out.

This passion for sweet things is said to have originated with the seafaring Venetians, who were the first to import cane sugar from the Orient. In fact, they were also responsible for the introduction of coffee and spices, which play a major part in many Italian desserts.

Venice may have been an important influence on Italian cuisine over the centuries, but so too were the Arabs, who ruled in the south of Italy, particularly in Sicily, for decades. They introduced a multitude of trees, fruits and nuts from their homelands – chief among them being citrus fruit, figs and almonds – and these play a major role in many Italian puds, cakes and biscuits. But perhaps the most significant Arab influence was the concept of freezing, resulting in the *gelati*, or ice-creams, for which Italy is now so famous.

Christian traditions have also been responsible for many of Italy's sweet tastes. The Italians love to celebrate, and each and every event in the calendar – whether a saint's day, Easter, All Souls' Day or Christmas – is fêted, in various parts of the country, with a special sweet cake, tart or biscuit.

Not surprisingly given Italy's warm sun and fertile lands, fruit and nuts are at the heart of a great number of the country's sweet dishes. In fact, many Italians choose just a simple piece of fruit as their perfect pud. Whatever your preference, life will indeed be sweet if you try even a few of the recipes in the following pages.

Puddings

Most Italian meals end with fruit rather than with a more complicated pudding. But there are a number of classic puddings – some of them, such as pannacotta and zabaglione, very well known. Many Italian desserts involve cooking fruit – figs simmered in *Vin Santo*, poached pears coated with chocolate, or peaches baked with an almond-based filling, for instance. And there is a great tradition of preserving fruit, which can then be served, months afterwards, with ice-cream or mascarpone. The famous soft and fresh cheeses of Italy are also used a lot in puddings – in cheesecakes, for instance, or in *cassata*, often in tandem with Italian sponge. The classic Italian ingredients of nuts, chocolate and coffee all make an appearance in many different kinds of desserts. But whatever your taste, there is a host of recipes here, all of which would make a perfect ending to a special meal, and many of them are particularly popular at Christmas.

Marsala trifle

There are many variations of this popular dessert, which is served in restaurants throughout Italy. Loosely translated, the Italian name *zuppa Inglese* means 'English soup', but in fact this is a rich cream trifle, which is served mostly at Christmas.

SERVES 8

cake
3 eggs
115g (4oz) caster sugar
115g (4oz) plain white or '00' Italian flour
½ tsp baking powder
3 tbsp Marsala

crème anglaise
450ml (¾ pint) milk
4 egg yolks
85g (3oz) caster sugar
½ tsp salt
1 tsp pure vanilla extract
finely grated zest of ½ unwaxed lemon

topping
300ml (10fl oz) double cream
a few toasted flaked almonds, to decorate

1 Preheat the oven to 180°C/350°F/gas mark 4. Brush a 20cm (8in) springform cake tin thoroughly with a little melted butter.

2 Beat together the eggs and sugar for 10-15 minutes, until thick and creamy. Sift the flour and baking powder together then, using a metal spoon, fold into the egg mixture.

3 Spoon the mixture into the prepared tin and bake for 20 minutes, until the cake is golden and has shrunk away from the sides of the tin. Leave to cool in the tin.

4 When cool, remove the cake from the tin and break it up into bite-sized pieces. Place it in a large serving bowl or individual serving dishes. Pour over the Marsala and set aside.

5 Meanwhile, prepare the *crème anglaise*. In a saucepan, bring the milk to just below boiling point and keep it hot. In a bowl, whisk together the egg yolks, sugar and salt until pale and fluffy. Pour in the hot milk, stirring with a wooden spoon. Return the mixture to a clean pan and heat gently, stirring all the time, until the mixture thickens and coats the back of a wooden spoon. Stir in the vanilla extract and lemon zest, and pour over the cake. Leave until cold.

6 When cold, whip the cream until it holds its shape, then use to cover the crème anglaise. Scatter over the almonds to decorate.

Chocolate trifle

This recipe is more like a very rich chocolate mousse with brandy-soaked biscuits. It's quick to prepare and tastes even better eaten the next day.

SERVES 8

3 Italian lady's finger sponges or
   3 slices Italian sponge cake (see pages
   150 and 127)
2 tbsp brandy
175g (6oz) dark chocolate with 70%
   cocoa solids
40g (1½oz) unsalted butter
3 eggs, separated
85g (3oz) caster sugar
4 tbsp double cream
toasted flaked almonds, to decorate

1 Lay the lady's fingers or slices of Italian sponge cake in the bottom of a 20cm (8in) shallow, round serving dish. Pour over the brandy and leave to soak.

2 Meanwhile, break the chocolate into pieces and dice the butter. Melt the chocolate and butter together in a bowl over simmering water, then leave to cool.

3 Whisk together the egg yolks and sugar until thick and creamy, and add to the chocolate mixture. Whip the cream until stiff and fold it into the chocolate mixture. Lastly, whisk the egg whites until stiff and fold them into the chocolate mixture.

4 Pour into the serving dish on top of the sponges. Chill for at least 2-3 hours, or up to a day, in the fridge before serving, decorated with toasted almonds.

Hazelnut and citrus zest meringues

'Ugly but delicious' is the literal translation of the Italian name, *'brutti ma buone'*, for these exquisite flourless small cakes. They come out looking like unsightly lumps that are studded with chopped nuts.

1 Preheat the oven to 190°C/375°F/gas mark 5, and grease a 26 x 39cm (10½ x 15½in) baking sheet.

2 Put the nuts in a mixing bowl, add the zests, and stir in the sugar.

3 Whip the egg whites to stiff peaks, and gently fold them into the nut and zest mixture until well blended.

4 Using a teaspoon, drop a spoonful of the mixture at a time on to the prepared baking sheet. Leave 1cm (½in) free around each cake.

5 Bake for 20-25 minutes, until firm. Let the meringues cool and harden on the sheet. They can be stored in an air-tight jar for several weeks.

6 Serve 2 meringues sandwiched together with whipped cream and pieces of fresh seasonal fruits.

SERVES 6

250g (9oz) shelled hazelnuts, chopped
finely grated zest of 1 unwaxed lemon
finely grated zest of 1 unwaxed orange
85g (3oz) caster sugar
3 egg whites
whipped cream, to serve
pieces of seasonal fruits, to serve

Peaches and strawberries in Marsala

In Italy we have many different fruits to make the perfect ending to a meal. Sometimes the fruit is simply served bobbing in a bowl of water, for you to peel and eat. This dessert is more sophisticated and should be eaten when both peaches and strawberries are at their best.

1 Skin the peaches, remove the stones and slice the flesh. Remove the stems from the strawberries, wipe and slice in half.

2 In a bowl, gently mix together the peaches and strawberries, the sugar if using, and the wine. Cover and leave to marinate for 1 hour.

3 Serve in individual glass dishes and accompany with plain sweet biscuits.

SERVES 4

2 medium peaches
225g (8oz) ripe strawberries
1 tbsp icing sugar (optional)
4 tbsp Marsala

Apricots in sweet wine

Apricots make me think of two things: the approach of summer and my mother – she just adores them. I particularly like them when they have a blush on their skin, which is a sign that they are ripe and at their best.

1 Place the apricots in a large deep saucepan with all the remaining ingredients. Bring to the boil, then simmer gently for about 20 minutes.

2 Leave the apricots to cool in their juices.

3 Spoon into a serving dish, and serve with ice-cream.

SERVES 6

675g (1½lb) fresh apricots, stoned
   and halved
140g (5oz) caster sugar
1 tbsp lemon juice
1 x 750ml bottle sweet white wine

Figs in Vin Santo

Vin Santo is a strong, white dessert wine from Tuscany. The lemon cuts into the sweetness of the wine and figs, and balances the flavour. I cannot think of a better marriage, and the preserved figs are perfect at Christmas, served with ice-cream or mascarpone cheese.

SERVES 4-6

22 dried figs
250ml (9fl oz) *Vin Santo* or other sweet dessert wine
2 tbsp lemon juice
finely grated zest of 2 unwaxed lemons

1 Cut the tough tops off the figs. Put in a saucepan with the Vin Santo and heat to simmering point, then poach for about 15 minutes until tender. Add the lemon juice and zest, and stir well together. Leave to cool.

2 When cold, drain the figs, reserving the liquid. Pack the figs into air-tight jars and cover with the syrup.

3 Cover and store in a cool, dry, dark place for up to 18 months (if you can!).

Muscatel raisins in wine

A jar of these raisins makes a great Christmas present, and my father just loves them. Muscatel raisins are available from health-food shops. Preserved like this, they are always wonderful served with ice-cream.

MAKES ABOUT 450G (1IB)

300g (10½oz) Muscatel raisins
thickly pared zest of 3 unwaxed lemons
300ml (10fl oz) sweet white wine
4 tsp lemon juice
1 tbsp rum (optional)

1 Fill a jar with the raisins, add the lemon zest and cover with the wine, lemon juice and rum, if using. Cover and seal.

2 Leave for at least a week before using, to allow the fruit to absorb the alcohol. Store in a cool, dark place for up to a year.

Zabaglione

This is a most fabulous Sicilian pudding. The delicious foam is so rich that it is best accompanied by fresh fruit. It was once prescribed by Italian doctors as a pick-me-up, and was often eaten for breakfast. It really does produce a good, warm feeling.

SERVES 2

2 egg yolks
2 tbsp caster sugar
2 tbsp Marsala

1 Put the egg yolks and sugar in a large heatproof bowl, or in the top pan of a double boiler, and whisk together. When the mixture starts to thicken, place the bowl over a saucepan of gently simmering water.

2 Add the Marsala and whisk continuously until the mixture becomes thick, hot and foamy.

3 Spoon into serving dishes and serve at once.

Sicilian cassata

This is a simple, classic dessert, made from ricotta and sponge cake, and should not be confused with *cassata gelata*, which is an ice-cream bombe. Prepare it a day ahead of time.

1 Line the base and sides of a 1.7 litre (3 pint) pudding basin with clingfilm.

2 Beat together the ricotta and sugar until light and fluffy. Divide the mixture in half.

3 Chop half of the chocolate into small pieces. Add to one-half of the ricotta mixture with the cinnamon and Amaretto. Fold the pistachio nuts and glacé fruits through the other half. Cover both mixtures and set aside.

4 Use the lady's fingers to line the prepared bowl, pressing them firmly around the bowl so that they are even. Fill with the fruit ricotta mixture, then the chocolate ricotta mixture. Cover the top with the cake. Cover the bowl and freeze for 2 hours or longer.

5 Melt the remaining chocolate and pour over the top of the sponge in the bowl. Return to the freezer for about 15 minutes, until set.

6 To make the topping, whip the cream and Amaretto together until it just holds its shape.

7 Just before serving, turn out the *cassata*. Ease round the edges with a palette knife, then place a serving plate over the top. Invert the bowl on to the plate, and let the cassata gently ease out, chocolate-side down.

8 Spread over the cream mixture to cover, and decorate with glacé fruit.

SERVES 8-10

450g (1lb) ricotta
225g (8oz) caster sugar
225g (8oz) dark chocolate with 70% cocoa solids
½ tsp ground cinnamon
2 tbsp Amaretto
175g (6oz) shelled pistachio nuts, chopped
200g (7oz) glacé fruits, chopped
1 quantity Italian lady's finger sponges (see page 150)
½ Italian sponge cake (see page 127), cut horizontally

topping
225ml (8fl oz) double cream
1 tbsp Amaretto
glacé fruit, to decorate

Stuffed pears with a chocolate sauce

I can't think of a better culinary combination than pears and chocolate. Do use ripe pears – I like Williams pears for this particular dessert.

SERVES 6

1½ tbsp lemon juice
finely grated zest of 2 unwaxed lemons
300ml (10fl oz) freshly squeezed orange juice
600ml (1 pint) medium white wine
4 whole cloves
115g (4oz) caster sugar
6 ripe pears
90ml (3fl oz) double cream
75g (2¾oz) shelled hazelnuts, toasted and chopped

chocolate sauce
55g (2oz) dark chocolate with 70% cocoa solids
15g (½oz) unsalted butter

1 Put the lemon juice and zest, orange juice, wine, cloves and caster sugar in a large saucepan. Heat gently to dissolve the sugar.

2 Peel each pear, leaving the stems attached. Slice off the bottom off each pear so it will stand up. Remove the core from the bottom with a sharp knife. Stand the pears upright in the syrup in the saucepan. Simmer, covered, for 20 minutes, or until the fruit is tender.

3 Remove the pears from the syrup and leave to cool. Remove the cloves from the syrup and discard. Simmer the syrup for about 45 minutes, until well reduced, to about 200ml (7fl oz). The liquid will become much darker and thicker. Leave to cool.

4 When the pears have cooled, lay each one on its side. Using a small, sharp knife, slit the pears open down one side, leaving the stalks attached (the idea being to make a cavity in the middle).

5 Whip the cream until it holds its shape, then fold in the hazelnuts. Spoon the cream mixture into each pear hollow. Gently put the pears together again and stand upright in a serving dish.

6 To prepare the chocolate sauce, gently melt the chocolate and butter together in a small saucepan. Do not boil.

7 Pour a little of the syrup over each pear and serve the rest separately. Pour a little of the chocolate sauce over the top of the pears and serve.

Zuccotto

This traditional Tuscan trifle, which translates to English as 'little pumpkin', is recognised by the classical pattern on the icing sugar and cocoa decoration. It is particularly good when served the day after it's made. Keep in the fridge until served.

1 Line a 1.7 litre (3 pint) pudding basin with a circle of greaseproof paper and lightly grease with oil.

2 Break half of the chocolate into a heatproof bowl and stand the bowl over a saucepan of simmering water. Heat until melted, then remove the bowl from the heat. Chop the remaining chocolate into small pieces.

3 Roughly chop the almonds and hazelnuts. Whip the cream until it holds its shape, then mix in the chopped nuts and chopped chocolate.

4 Divide the cream in half and add the melted chocolate to one-half. Sift 55g (2oz) of the icing sugar into each half of the cream and stir in gently. Chill in the fridge until required.

5 Slice the crust off the top of the cake half. Push the cake into the bowl and ease it up to line the sides.

6 Mix together the rum, brandy and cherry brandy. Brush the cake with the rum mixture to moisten it completely and help it to fit the bowl firmly. Trim off any untidy edges and use your hands to get as smooth a finish as you can.

7 Spoon in the white cream mixture and spread it evenly up the sides. Fill the centre with the chocolate mixture and smooth the top. Cover and place in the fridge for at least 2 hours before serving.

8 Cut out a circle of greaseproof paper about the same size as the *zuccotto* when turned out. Draw on it 8 even wedges, and cut out each alternate wedge.

9 To serve, turn the *zuccotto* out on to a serving plate. Sift the remaining icing sugar over the whole top. Place the cut-out paper over the top and liberally sift the cocoa over. Carefully remove the paper and you will have adorned the *zuccotto* with its classical design.

SERVES 10-12

280g (10oz) dark chocolate with 70% cocoa solids
85g (3oz) blanched almonds, toasted
85g (3oz) blanched hazelnuts, toasted
1 litre (1¾ pints) whipping cream
140g (5oz) icing sugar
½ Italian sponge cake (see page 127), cut horizontally
3 tbsp each of rum, brandy and cherry brandy
2 tbsp cocoa powder

Chocolate mousse

This mousse has an almost chocolate-truffle-type consistency, and is very, very rich. The recipe was given to me by my friend Claudio, who lives in Perugia.

SERVES 6-8

175g (6oz) dark chocolate with 70% cocoa solids
450ml (16fl oz) whipping cream
2 eggs, separated
55g (2oz) shelled hazelnuts, toasted and chopped

1 Break the chocolate into pieces and put in a heatproof bowl over a saucepan of barely simmering water. As soon as the chocolate has melted, remove the bowl from the heat and leave until it has cooled but is still liquid.

2 Whip the cream until it just holds its shape. Fold in the beaten egg yolks. Whisk the egg whites until stiff but not dry.

3 Fold the cream into the chocolate, followed by the chopped hazelnuts. Lastly, fold in the egg whites.

4 Spoon into a serving dish and chill in the fridge for 4 hours before serving.

Chestnut and chocolate puddings

The sweet chestnut tree is found all over Italy and has been called the ultimate in organic food as it grows solely with the help of rainwater and sunlight. In Italy, we often cook chestnuts with bay leaves for the mild flavour the latter impart.

1 If using fresh chestnuts, pierce each one, put in a saucepan with the bay leaves and cover with water. Bring to the boil and simmer for 25 minutes, until tender. Drain and, as soon as they are cool enough to handle, remove the shells and skin. Put in a food processor and blend to form a purée.

2 Put the chocolate, sugar, butter, vanilla and rum in a saucepan. Heat gently until the sugar has dissolved, then add the fresh or canned chestnut purée. Remove from the heat and mix together until the ingredients are well blended. Pour into a large bowl and leave to cool.

3 Whip the cream until it just holds its shape, then fold into the cooled mixture. Spoon the mixture into 8 ramekin dishes and chill in the fridge for 2-3 hours, until firm and set.

4 Serve topped with a little cream and a dusting of sifted cocoa powder, if you like.

SERVES 8

675g (1½lb) fresh chestnuts, or 1 x 435g
    can unsweetened chestnut purée
3 bay leaves (if using fresh chestnuts)
175g (6oz) dark chocolate with 70%
    cocoa solids
175g (6oz) caster sugar
175g (6oz) unsalted butter
½ tsp pure vanilla extract
50ml (2fl oz) dark rum
200ml (7fl oz) double cream
whipped cream and cocoa powder, to
    serve (optional)

Apostle's fingers

These fingers are carefully rolled pancakes with a fresh ricotta and chocolate filling. When they have been cut, they really do resemble fingers.

MAKES 24 FINGERS

batter
5 eggs
25g (1oz) caster sugar
115g (4oz) plain white or '00' Italian flour
pinch of salt
225ml (8fl oz) milk
unsalted butter, for greasing

filling
450g (1lb) ricotta
175g (6oz) caster sugar
grated zest of 1 unwaxed lemon
grated zest of 1 unwaxed orange
grated zest of 1 unwaxed clementine
 (optional)
1 tbsp double cream
55g (2oz) dark chocolate with 70%
 cocoa solids
2 tbsp rum
candied zest, to decorate

1 To prepare the batter, whisk together the eggs and sugar until well blended. Beat in the flour, add the salt and gradually add the milk, whisking vigorously until the batter is smooth. Cover and leave to stand for 30-60 minutes.

2 To make the filling, put the ricotta in a bowl and beat in the sugar, zests and cream until smooth. Finely chop the chocolate and beat into the mixture with the rum.

3 Wipe a heavy, 28cm (11in) non-stick crêpe pan with a little butter. Place over a medium heat. When the pan is medium hot, ladle in enough batter to cover the base. Cook until it bubbles and the underside is golden brown, then turn and cook the other side until golden brown. Remove from the pan and stack on a large plate, interleaved with greaseproof paper. Repeat with the remaining batter to make 8 pancakes.

4 Lay a pancake on a work-surface and cut away any brittle edges. Place a heaped tablespoon of the filling in the middle, then spread very thinly over the whole pancake. Roll the pancake tightly towards you. Repeat with each pancake. Slice each across at a slight diagonal into 3 fingers. Discard the ends of each roll.

5 Chill in the fridge before serving. If wished, decorate with candied zest and eat with your fingers.

Caramel panna cotta

Panna cotta has gained worldwide popularity. This is an old recipe from Piedmont, which contains rum and Marsala.

1 Preheat the oven to 120°C/250°F/gas mark ½. Warm a 23 x 13cm (9 x 5in) loaf tin in the oven while making the syrup.

2 For the syrup, heat the sugar in a small, heavy-based saucepan over a medium-to-low heat. Do not stir until the sugar begins to melt around the pan. Stir with a wooden spoon until the sugar dissolves into a smooth syrup that is nutty brown in colour. Quickly pour the caramel syrup into the warm loaf tin and rotate the tin every way to coat the entire surface. The syrup will be very hot, so be sure to wear protective oven mitts when holding the saucepan and when coating the loaf tin. Set the tin on a wire rack to cool completely. The caramel will harden and crack.

3 For the *panna cotta*, pour 4 tbsp of the milk into a small bowl, sprinkle over the gelatine and set aside. The gelatine will become spongy in texture. Scald the remaining milk in a small saucepan over a medium heat. Remove from the heat and add the gelatine mixture. Stir until dissolved.

4 In another saucepan, combine the cream with the icing sugar, and warm over a medium heat. Stir constantly with a wooden spoon until the cream is very warm and the sugar has completely dissolved. Pour the cream mixture into a large bowl, and combine it with the milk and gelatine mixture. Leave to cool completely.

5 When the cream is cool, stir in the rum, Marsala and vanilla. Pour the mixture through a strainer into the caramel-lined loaf tin. Refrigerate the pan overnight until the *panna cotta* becomes firm.

6 Unmould when you are ready to serve. Slice the *panna cotta*, and spoon some of the caramel syrup over each slice.

SERVES 6

caramel syrup
140g (5oz) caster sugar

pannacotta
400ml (14fl oz) milk
2½ tsp powdered gelatine
500ml (18fl oz) double cream
100g (3½oz) icing sugar
2 tbsp white rum
1 tbsp dry Marsala
1½ tsp pure vanilla extract

Panna cotta

This dessert is eaten mainly in the north of Italy, where dairy products are used a lot. It is very rich, so servings are small, and I like to serve it with a purée of apricots that have been soaked in brandy and lemon juice.

1 Put the cream, sugar and vanilla extract in a saucepan and simmer for 2-3 minutes.

2 Dissolve the agar agar in about 2 tbsp warm water. Beat well into the cream.

3 Pour into a small serving bowl or 4 individual bowls or ramekin dishes. Chill in the fridge for 2-3 hours before serving.

SERVES 4

300ml (10fl oz) double cream
2 tbsp caster sugar, or more to taste
8 drops pure vanilla extract
2 tsp agar agar or 1 tbsp powdered
  gelatine

Roman cheesecake

I first enjoyed this recipe in Rome when my colleagues and I stumbled across an excellent café. The cheesecake is light, yet rich and creamy, and so easy to make.

SERVES 8

unsalted butter, for greasing
2 tbsp fresh white breadcrumbs
55g (2oz) dried apricots, or 115g (4oz)
   fresh apricots
2 tbsp seedless raisins
50ml (2fl oz) Marsala or Amaretto
675g (1½lb) ricotta
115g (4oz) runny honey
2 eggs, separated
finely grated zest of 1 unwaxed lemon

1 Preheat the oven to 180°C/350°F/gas mark 4. Generously butter the base and sides of a 20cm (8in) springform or loose-bottomed cake tin. Dust with the breadcrumbs, covering both base and sides as evenly as possible.

2 Finely chop the dried or fresh apricots. Soak the raisins, and the dried apricots if using, in the liqueur for 30 minutes.

3 Sieve the ricotta into a large bowl and beat in the honey and egg yolks. Stir in the soaked fruits and their liqueur, the apricots (if using) and the lemon zest.

4 Whisk the egg whites until they are stiff but not dry, then fold them into the cheese mixture.

5 Pour into the prepared tin and bake for 50-60 minutes, until a skewer inserted in the centre comes out clean. Cool in the tin for 2-3 minutes, then remove from the tin and transfer to a wire cake rack, still on its base, and leave to cool completely.

Lemon mascarpone cheesecake

This popular dessert is very easy to make. It can be made with ricotta instead of mascarpone if you wish, and can be served with fresh strawberries or raspberries when they are in season.

1 Preheat the oven to 180°C/350°F/gas mark 4. Generously butter the base and sides of a deep, 20cm (8in) loose-bottomed cake tin.

2 Melt the butter. Crush the amaretti biscuits, then mix the crumbs with the melted butter. Put in the bottom of the prepared cake tin.

3 Put the mascarpone, lemon zest and juice, sugar and egg yolks in a bowl and, using a wooden spoon, mix together. Sprinkle the cornflour over the top and fold in.

4 In a separate bowl, whisk the egg whites with the salt until stiff. Fold into the cheese mixture. Spread the mixture into the cake tin and smooth the top.

5 Bake for 35 minutes, until firm to the touch. Leave to cool in the tin.

SERVES 8

85g (3oz) unsalted butter, plus extra for greasing
175g (6oz) amaretti biscuits
400g (14oz) mascarpone
finely grated zest of 3 unwaxed lemons and juice of 1
115g (4oz) caster sugar
2 eggs, separated
2 tbsp cornflour
pinch of salt

Coffee ricotta

Ricotta has many uses in both sweet and savoury dishes. It is a by-product of cheese-making, made from the whey, and it varies in flavour depending on whether full-cream or skimmed milk is added. I love its cool, creamy texture and, as I'm addicted to coffee, this recipe is a real favourite for me.

1 Sieve the ricotta into a bowl. Add the remaining ingredients and stir together until smooth.

2 Place in a serving dish and leave in the fridge for at least 2½ hours for the flavours to develop.

3 Serve with fresh cream and Twice-baked cookies (see page 158).

SERVES 4

280g (10oz) ricotta
115g (4oz) golden caster sugar
2 tbsp finely ground coffee
2 tbsp rum
1 tsp vanilla extract
double cream, to serve

Stuffed peaches

There are not many old Italian desserts, but this is one of the classics. It is Sergio Torelli's recipe; he's the head chef at Savini's, Milan's famous restaurant near the Duomo.

SERVES 6

25g (1oz) unsalted butter, plus extra for greasing
6 yellow peaches
115g (4oz) whole blanched almonds
12 amaretti biscuits
55g (2oz) caster sugar
1 egg yolk
2 tbsp Marsala, Maraschino (cherry liqueur) or Amaretto
finely grated zest of ½ unwaxed lemon
50ml (2fl oz) white wine
icing sugar, to serve

1 Preheat the oven to 180°C/350°F/gas mark 4. Butter a shallow ovenproof dish.

2 Cut the peaches in half and remove the stones. Place the halves in the prepared dish, cut-side up.

3 Put the almonds and amaretti biscuits in a food processor and coarsely grind. Mix in the caster sugar, egg yolk, Marsala and lemon zest.

4 Use this mixture to stuff the peach halves, piling it up slightly. Sprinkle the wine over, and place a shaving of extra butter on top of each peach half.

5 Bake for about 20 minutes, until the peaches are soft but still holding their shape. Serve dusted with sifted icing sugar.

Apple bread pudding

This pudding is made with bread, but you would get great results by using slices of the fruit cake ring on page 123.

1 Put 85g (3oz) of the sugar and 125ml (4fl oz) water in a saucepan. Heat gently until the sugar has dissolved, then bring to the boil and heat for about 5 minutes, until it turns a caramel colour. Immediately and carefully pour the caramel into a 23cm (9in) deep ring mould and swirl to coat the bottom of the mould. Leave to set.

2 Put the raisins in a small bowl, cover with the brandy, and leave to marinate for 30 minutes.

3 Put the bread or cake in a large dish and pour over the milk. Set aside. Meanwhile, core, peel and thinly slice the apples.

4 Preheat the oven to 180°C/350°F/gas mark 4.

5 In a large bowl, whisk together the remaining sugar with the eggs, salt and butter until well blended. Add the raisins with their brandy, plus the apple slices. Drain the soaked bread, add to the mixture and mix the ingredients together by hand.

6 Pour the apple and bread mixture into the mould, spreading it in evenly. Place the mould in a roasting tin and fill the tin with enough boiling water to come 4cm (1½in) up the sides. Bake for 45 minutes, until set.

7 Remove the mould from the tin, let it stand for 2 minutes, then place a serving dish over the top of the mould and carefully invert the pudding on to it. Shake and release the pudding, including its sauce. Serve warm, cut into wedges.

SERVES 6-8

175g (6oz) caster sugar
85g (3oz) raisins
2-3 tbsp brandy
12 slices day-old bread or cake
350ml (12fl oz) milk
5 apples
3 eggs
pinch of salt
85g (3oz) unsalted butter

Orange soufflé

This '*sformato*' is not unlike a soufflé, but it has the texture of a pudding. It is a very old dish that was originally served at banquets in the 17th-century, and today is mainly cooked in Italian homes rather than in restaurants.

SERVES 10

3 medium juicy unwaxed oranges
1 tsp coarse-grained salt
225g (8oz) blanched almonds, finely chopped
55g (2oz) broken walnuts, finely chopped
6 extra large eggs, separated
225g (8oz) caster sugar
1 tsp orange-flower water

to finish and decorate
115g (4oz) granulated sugar
2 tsp lemon juice
50ml (2fl oz) light rum
115g (4oz) blanched almonds, toasted and roughly chopped
225ml (8fl oz) double cream
2 tbsp caster sugar
1 tsp icing sugar
shredded zest of 1 unwaxed orange, to decorate

1 Put the whole oranges in a large bowl. Add 1.2 litres (2 pints) cold water and the salt and leave to soak for 1 hour.

2 Drain and wash the oranges, then put them in a small saucepan with 1.2 litres (2 pints) fresh cold water. (The oranges should be completely covered by the water.) Put the pan over a medium heat. Bring to the boil, cover and simmer for 45 minutes. Drain and leave the oranges to cool.

3 When cool, cut the oranges in half and remove the pips. Put the oranges in a food processor and blend until smooth. Pour into a bowl. Add the finely chopped almonds and walnuts.

4 Preheat the oven to 200°C/400°F/gas mark 6. Butter and lightly flour a 22cm (8½in) soufflé dish.

5 Put the egg yolks and caster sugar in a bowl and whisk until thick and creamy. Add the orange-flower water and mix well. Pour the mixture into the bowl with the oranges and nuts, and mix well.

6 Whisk the egg whites until stiff but not dry, then fold into the mixture. Turn the mixture into the prepared dish and bake for 1 hour, until firm to the touch and a skewer inserted in the centre comes out clean. Remove from the oven and leave to stand for an hour.

7 To make a syrup, put 225ml (8fl oz) water and the granulated sugar in a small saucepan. Put the pan over a low heat until the sugar has dissolved, then bring to the boil, add the lemon juice and simmer for 10 minutes, until a thick syrup is formed.

8 Meanwhile, line a cake stand with baking parchment and turn the soufflé out on to it. Pour the rum over the soufflé. Brush the syrup on the sides of the soufflé to moisten, then cover the sides with the chopped almonds. Leave to stand for 5 minutes so the almonds become attached to the soufflé.

9 Whisk the cream until it just holds its shape, then add the caster and icing sugars. Transfer the soufflé to a serving plate. Spoon the whipped cream on top to decorate and sprinkle over the orange shreds.

Chocolate and banana basket

This is an Italian take on the famous banoffi pie. The recipe came from my aunt in Italy, who is very excited that I am putting it in my book.

1 Make a hole in the condensed milk can and cook in a bain-marie for 2½ hours, simmering gently until the milk coming out from the can is brown and caramel-like. Constantly control the level of water, adding some if needed. Leave the can to cool.

2 Open the can, and pour the contents into a bowl.

3 For the base, carefully butter a loose-bottomed tart mould of about 20cm (8in) in diameter, and with medium-high sides.

4 Melt the butter for the base, and leave it to cool down a little. Crush the biscuits by hand or in a processor, and mix with the melted butter. Coat the buttered mould with the biscuit mixture

5 Break the chocolate into pieces and melt in a bain-marie, stirring constantly, until it is completely melted. Leave it to cool down, then add 115g (4oz) of the whipped cream and the vanilla. Pour the chocolate cream on to the cold cake base and cover with the caramelized condensed milk.

6 Peel the bananas, cut into slices and cook in a little butter over a low heat until brown. Cover with the sugar and rum, and cook on a high heat for 1 minute. Remove from the heat. Leave to cool.

7 Lay the cold slices of bananas on top of the pudding. Put the remaining whipped cream into a piping bag fitted with a nozzle. Pipe over the top of the pudding.

SERVES 6-8

1 x 397ml can condensed milk
115g (4oz) plain chocolate, with 70% cocoa solids
175g (6oz) double cream, whipped
2 tsp pure vanilla extract
350g (12oz) ripe bananas
a little unsalted butter
55g (2oz) caster sugar
100ml (3½fl oz) white rum

base
115g (4oz) unsalted butter, plus extra for greasing
225g (8oz) digestive biscuits

Honey balls

We particularly eat these at Christmas time, but I wouldn't limit their enjoyment to once a year. Children just love them.

SERVES 4

225g (8oz) plain white or '00' Italian flour
25g (1oz) unsalted butter
140g (5oz) caster sugar
2 eggs, lightly beaten
about 1 tbsp dry white wine
plenty of olive oil, for deep-frying
115g (4oz) fragrant honey

1 Using a fork, mix together the flour, butter, 25g (1oz) of the sugar, the eggs and the wine to make a soft dough. Add 1 tsp extra wine, if needed.

2 On a lightly floured surface, lightly knead the dough, then pinch off pieces about the size of a chestnut and roll into balls. This quantity of dough will make about 20 small balls.

3 Heat the olive oil until just beginning to lightly smoke. Fry the dough balls, a few at a time, in the hot oil until they are golden, about 4 minutes. Drain on kitchen paper.

4 In a small saucepan, slowly heat the remaining sugar and the honey to form a caramel, taking care not to let the mixture boil.

5 On a serving dish, pile the balls into a pyramid, pour over the honey caramel sauce and turn the balls to coat. Serve immediately, with a little extra sauce poured over.

Italian doughnuts

These cakes are similar to doughnuts, and they are wonderful served with a glass of sparkling Prosecco.

SERVES 4-6

225g (8oz) strong white flour
15g (½oz) fresh yeast, dissolved in 75ml
   (2½fl oz) warm water
85g (3oz) caster sugar
100ml (3½fl oz) white wine
finely grated zest of 1 unwaxed lemon
55g (2oz) sultanas
sunflower oil, for frying
icing sugar, for dusting

1 Mix all the ingredients together, except for the oil and icing sugar, and beat well into a smooth batter. Let this rest for 1 hour in a warm (not hot) place.

2 Put a deep pan of sunflower oil on to heat and test for temperature by dribbling a little of the batter into it. If it sizzles and turns golden, the oil is ready.

3 Drop the batter into the oil in spoonfuls, taking care not to overcrowd the pan. When the doughnuts are golden brown, after about 4 minutes, remove and drain well on kitchen paper. Serve hot with a light dusting of icing sugar.

Fried apple slices

I like to use Cox's orange pippins or Braeburn apples for this recipe. You could even marinade the apples in brandy.

SERVES 4

1 tsp fresh yeast, dissolved in 100ml (3½fl
   oz) warm water
125g (4½oz) caster sugar
1 large egg, beaten
300ml (½ pint) olive oil, for frying, plus
   3 tbsp
100ml (3½fl oz) dry white wine
225g (8oz) plain white or '00' Italian flour
¼ tsp salt
4 eating apples

1 Mix 2 tbsp of the caster sugar, the beaten egg, 3 tbsp olive oil and the wine into the yeast mixture and combine well.

2 Sift the flour and salt into a large bowl. Make a well in the centre, add the yeast mixture, and whisk until it has the consistency of a pancake batter. If the batter seems too stiff, add a little more wine or water.

3 Peel, core and slice each apple into 5 rings. In a deep, heavy-based saucepan, heat the remaining olive oil – it is ready when a bit of batter dropped into the oil sizzles and browns. Coat a few apple slices on both sides with the batter, letting the excess drain off. Fry the slices for 3-4 minutes, until golden. Drain on kitchen paper. Cook the remaining slices in the same way.

4 Put the remaining caster sugar on a plate. When the apple slices are cool enough to handle, gently press them into the sugar. Serve warm.

Mrs Ferrigno's meringues

My mother makes the best meringues I've ever tasted. They are crisp on the outside and chewy on the inside. My mother will say it's the Aga that produces such good results, but I know it's because she is so particular at every stage of making them. Meringues are popular in Italy, eaten plain, with fruit or cream.

1 Preheat the oven to 150°C/300°F/gas mark 2. Line 2 or more baking trays with baking parchment.

2 In a large, clean bowl, whisk together the egg whites and salt until thick and creamy. Add half the sugar and continue whisking. Gradually fold in the remaining sugar. The mixture should be stiff and opaque.

3 Form individual nests or rounds on the prepared trays. To make the nests, dollop 6 spoonfuls on to the tray and make a hollow in the centre. For the filled meringues, spoon on 20 much smaller blobs. Bake for 1½ hours, until dry. Turn over and bake for a further 45 minutes. They will have changed colour and become deep golden. Leave to cool on a wire rack.

4 To serve, either sandwich the small meringues with whipped cream or make the bigger ones into fruit-filled nests with cream.

MAKES 10 FILLED MERINGUES
AND 6 NESTS

4 egg whites, at room temperature
pinch of salt
225g (8oz) caster sugar

to serve
double cream, whipped
small pieces of fresh fruit (optional)

Tarts and pastries

Every *pasticceria* in Italy has a window filled with a tantalising, colourful array of tarts and pastries. The Italians buy a slice to go with their morning espresso or to have as an afternoon *merenda* (the equivalent of high tea), or they buy a whole tart to take home to serve as a dessert. Some of the smaller pastries can even be eaten for breakfast (well, I do!). The pastry used is a basic sweet shortcrust, made with '00' Italian flour, butter, egg and sugar, but often it has the added tang and texture of ground nuts, vanilla or grated lemon zest. The fillings are principally the fruits that grow so prolifically in Italy – peaches, figs, apricots, cherries, lemons, raspberries – but there are nut tarts and jam tarts too. Smaller sweet pastries are an Italian speciality, and they range from the famous Sicilian *cannoli* to the little ricotta, jam or custard tarts of Naples.

Fig and lemon tart

This tart is best made with the *madonna* fig, which is the first fig of the year, picked at the end of May. The tart is very moist and so it should ideally be eaten on the day it is made.

SERVES 10-12

pastry
225g (8oz) plain white or '00' Italian flour,
   plus extra for dusting
1 tsp pure vanilla extract
115g (4oz) caster sugar
115g (4oz) unsalted butter, softened
1 egg yolk
1 tsp salt

filling
6 unwaxed lemons
115g (4oz) caster sugar
1kg (2¼lb) fresh figs, washed
1 tsp fennel seed

1 To make the pastry, put the flour in a bowl and make a well in the centre. Add the vanilla extract, sugar, butter, egg yolk and salt. Gradually work in the flour from the edges and mix to form a smooth dough. Wrap in greaseproof paper and chill in the fridge for 20 minutes.

2 Using a skewer, prick the skins of the lemons well. Put into a saucepan, add enough water to just cover, bring to the boil and boil for 10 minutes. Repeat this boiling process 3 times, changing the water each time.

3 Drain the lemons, reserving the last lot of water. Finely slice the lemons, leaving on the skin. Put the lemon slices in a saucepan with the sugar and the reserved water. Cover and cook over a low heat for about 10 minutes, until the liquid has reduced to about 150ml (5fl oz) and is syrupy. Drain off the syrup and reserve.

4 Preheat the oven to 180°C/350°F/gas mark 4.

5 On a lightly floured surface, roll out the pastry and use to line a greased 28cm (11in) loose-bottomed flan tin. Roll the rolling pin over the edges of the tin to remove excess pastry. With a fork, prick the base all over. Cover the dough with the lemon slices. Slice the figs and arrange on top. Pour the lemon syrup over the figs and sprinkle with the fennel seed.

6 Bake for 45 minutes, until the pastry is golden. Leave to cool before serving.

Peach and mascarpone tart

This delicious tart is enjoyed in Sicily when the peaches are ripe. The pastry is a dream!

SERVES 8

pastry
150g (5½oz) plain white or '00' Italian
    flour, plus extra for dusting
55g (2oz) icing sugar
3 tbsp ground almonds
½ tsp baking powder
pinch of salt
115g (4oz) unsalted butter, chilled
1 egg, beaten

filling
225g (8oz) mascarpone
55g (2oz) icing sugar
finely grated zest of 1 unwaxed orange
1 tsp pure vanilla extract
125ml (4fl oz) double cream
4 large ripe peaches
3 tbsp apricot conserve

1 To make the pastry, mix the flour, icing sugar, almonds, baking powder and salt together in a large bowl. Dice the butter, add to the flour and rub it in until the mixture resembles fine breadcrumbs. Make a well in the centre. Add the egg and gradually work in the flour from the edges, mixing to form a smooth dough.

2 On a lightly floured surface, roll out the pastry and use to line a greased 24cm (9½in) loose-bottomed flan tin. Roll the rolling pin over the edges of the tin to remove any excess pastry. With a fork, prick the base all over. Cover and chill in the fridge for 30 minutes.

3 Preheat the oven to 190°C/375°F/gas mark 5.

4 Line the pastry case with greaseproof paper and weigh down with baking beans. Blind-bake for 15 minutes, until the sides are crisp. Remove the lining and beans and return to the oven for 5 minutes, until golden brown. Trim the edges and leave to cool.

5 To make the filling, mix the mascarpone, icing sugar, orange zest and vanilla extract in a bowl. Whip the cream until it holds its shape, then fold into the mascarpone mixture.

6 Peel, stone and thinly slice the peaches. Spread the filling mixture in the pastry case and top with the peach slices. Melt the apricot conserve and brush over the peach slices to glaze. Chill, covered, in the fridge for 1 hour before serving.

Apricot and almond tart

My mother and grandmother have passed on to me their love of apricots. Their bright orange flesh is irresistible, either on its own or in this tart.

1 To make the pastry, sift the flour, salt, cornflour and icing sugar into a bowl. Dice the butter, add to the flour and rub it in until the mixture resembles fine breadcrumbs. Make a well in the centre. Add the egg yolk and 2 tbsp cold water, and gradually work in the flour from the edges to bind the ingredients together. Knead very lightly.

2 On a lightly floured surface, roll out the pastry and use to line a greased 23cm (9in) fluted, loose-bottomed flan tin. Roll the rolling pin over the edges of the tin to remove any excess pastry. With a fork, prick the base all over. Cover and chill in the fridge for 20 minutes.

3 Preheat the oven to 190°C/375°F/gas mark 5.

4 Line the pastry case with greaseproof paper and weigh down with baking beans. Blind-bake for 15 minutes, until the sides are crisp. Remove the lining and beans, and return to the oven for 5 minutes, until the base is crisp. Trim the edges.

5 To make the filling, put the icing sugar, eggs, egg yolk, ground almonds and lemon zest and juice in a bowl and mix well together. Pour into the flan case.

6 Cut the apricots in half, remove the stones, then arrange in the flan case with the skin-side down. Sprinkle over the flaked almonds.

7 Bake for about 35 minutes, until the filling is firm and golden. Dust with sifted icing sugar. Serve hot or cold, with cream if wished.

SERVES 8

pastry
225g (8oz) plain white or '00' Italian flour, plus extra for dusting
pinch of salt
25g (1oz) cornflour
2 tsp icing sugar
115g (4oz) unsalted butter
1 egg yolk

filling
115g (4oz) icing sugar
2 eggs plus 1 egg yolk
85g (3oz) ground almonds
finely grated zest and juice of 1 unwaxed lemon
8 ripe apricots
25g (1oz) flaked almonds

to serve
icing sugar, for dusting
double cream, to serve (optional)

Strawberry tart

This tart is typical of Italy and found in many *pasticcerie*. Use this recipe to experiment with different fruits when in season – my father loves it with whole black cherries and cherry conserve.

SERVES 6-8

pastry

300g (10½oz) plain white or '00' Italian
   flour, plus extra for dusting

pinch of salt

150g (5½oz) unsalted butter, softened

115g (4oz) caster sugar

1 egg

3 egg yolks

finely grated zest of 1 unwaxed lemon

filling and to serve

275g (10oz) strawberry conserve with a
   high fruit content

450g (1lb) strawberries

icing sugar, for dusting

1 To make the pastry, put the flour and salt into a bowl with the butter, sugar, egg, egg yolks and lemon zest. Using your fingertips, knead the ingredients together to form a soft dough. Wrap in greaseproof paper and chill in the fridge for 30 minutes.

2 Preheat the oven to 190°C/375°F/gas mark 5.

3 On a lightly floured surface, roll out three-quarters of the pastry and use it to line a greased 24cm (9½in) loose-bottomed flan tin. Roll the rolling pin over the edges of the tin remove any excess pastry. Spread the base with the strawberry conserve.

4 Roll out the remaining pastry, cut into strips and use to form a lattice on top of the conserve.

5 Bake for 20-25 minutes, until golden. Leave to cool in the tin. Before serving, decorate with whole strawberries and dust with sifted icing sugar.

Cherry and hazelnut tart

Cherries are in season in May and June and, as a change from eating them as fresh fruit, this recipe is a good way of using them Do use ripe, unblemished cherries. Hazelnuts give the pastry a rich taste and texture.

SERVES 12

pastry
200g (7oz) plain white or '00' Italian flour,
    plus extra for dusting
pinch of salt
140g (5oz) unsalted butter, chilled
85g (3oz) icing sugar
55g (2oz) shelled hazelnuts, toasted
    and chopped
1 egg yolk

filling
350g (12oz) mascarpone
25g (1oz) icing sugar
675g (1½lb) ripe cherries, pitted
2 tsp pure vanilla extract
1 tbsp brandy

1   To make the pastry, sift the flour and salt into a bowl. Dice the butter, add it to the flour and rub in with your fingertips until the mixture resembles fine breadcrumbs. Stir in the icing sugar and hazelnuts. Make a well in the centre. Add the egg yolk and about 2 tsp water and gradually work in the flour from the edges, mixing to form a smooth dough. Wrap in greaseproof paper and chill in the fridge for 30 minutes.

2   Meanwhile, stone the cherries, and preheat the oven to 190°C/375°F/gas mark 5.

3   On a lightly floured surface, roll out the pastry and use it to line a greased 28cm (11in) loose-bottomed flan tin. Roll the rolling pin over the edges of the tin to remove any excess pastry. With a fork, price the base all over. Line the pastry case with greaseproof paper and weigh down with baking beans. Blind-bake for 15 minutes, until the sides are crisp. Remove the lining and beans and return to the oven for 5 minutes, until the base is crisp.

4   In a large bowl, combine the mascarpone with the icing sugar, cherries, vanilla extract and brandy. Spoon into the cooked pastry case and serve.

Raspberry and almond tart

This tart is rich and succulent, with the raspberries enclosed in crisp pastry.

1 To make the pastry, sift the flour into a large bowl. Dice the butter, add it to the flour, and rub it in until the mixture resembles fine breadcrumbs. Stir in the sugar, cinnamon, lemon zest and ground almonds. Make a well in the centre. Add the egg yolks and mix with a round-bladed knife until the mixture binds together. Gather the mixture with one hand to form a smooth dough. Wrap in greaseproof paper and chill in the fridge for 1 hour.

2 Preheat the oven to 190°C/375°F/gas mark 5.

3 On a lightly floured surface, roll out the pastry and use to line a greased 23cm (9in) loose-bottomed flan tin. Roll the rolling pin over the edges of the tin to remove any excess pastry. With a fork, prick the base all over. Line the pastry case with greaseproof paper and weigh down with baking beans. Blind-bake for 15 minutes, until the sides of the pastry are crisp. Remove the lining and beans. Lightly beat the egg white and brush a little over the base of the flan. Return to the oven for 5 minutes, until the base is crisp.

4 Mix the conserve with the raspberries and spoon into the pastry case. Level the top with a palette knife. Brush the rim of the pastry case with egg white.

5 Roll out the pastry trimmings and cut into long, thin strips with a sharp knife or pastry cutter. Arrange the strips carefully across the filling to form a lattice pattern. Brush the pastry with the remaining beaten egg white and sprinkle over the sugar. Bake for 25-30 minutes, until golden brown.

SERVES 8-12

pastry
115g (4oz) plain white or '00' Italian flour, plus extra for dusting
85g (3oz) unsalted butter, chilled and cubed
85g (3oz) caster sugar
1 tsp ground cinnamon
finely grated zest of 1 unwaxed lemon
85g (3oz) ground almonds
2 egg yolks, beaten
1 egg white

filling
8 tbsp raspberry conserve with a high fruit content
225g (8oz) fresh or frozen raspberries
a little caster sugar

CROSTAT
€. 1,20 C

Orange tart

This is another citrus fruit recipe from Sicily, where oranges are sweet, juicy and plentiful.

1 To make the filling, pour the orange juice into a saucepan and boil gently until reduced to 225ml (8fl oz). Leave the juice to cool slightly while you make the pastry.

2 To make the pastry, sift the flour into a bowl. Dice the butter, add it to the flour and rub it in until the mixture resembles fine breadcrumbs. Add the sugar and egg and blend until the mixture forms into a ball.

3 On a lightly floured surface, roll out the pastry and use to line a greased 20cm (8in) deep-sided, loose-bottomed, fluted flan tin. Roll the rolling pin over the edges of the tin to remove any excess pastry. With a fork, prick the base all over. Cover and chill in the fridge for 30 minutes.

4 Preheat the oven to 190°C/375°F/gas mark 5.

5 Put the tart tin on a baking tray, line with greaseproof paper and weigh down with baking beans. Blind-bake for 15 minutes, until the sides are crisp. Remove the lining and beans and bake for a further 5 minutes, until the base is crisp.

6 Reduce the temperature of the oven to 180°C/350°F/gas mark 4.

7 Whisk together the cooled orange juice, orange zest, eggs, sugar and cream until well mixed, then pour into the pre-baked pastry case. Bake for 35 minutes, until softly set. Leave to cool before serving with crème fraîche.

SERVES 8

pastry
225g (8oz) plain white or '00' Italian flour,
    plus extra for dusting
115g (4oz) unsalted butter, chilled
2 tbsp caster sugar
1 egg

filling
1 litre (1¾ pints) freshly squeezed
    orange juice
finely grated zest of 4 unwaxed oranges
8 eggs
350g (12oz) caster sugar
225ml (8fl oz) double cream
crème fraîche, to serve

Sicilian lemon tart

This refreshing, tangy tart comes from Sicily. It is so good that you will be sure to want a second slice – fortunately it is large enough to go round!

SERVES 8

pastry
200g (7oz) plain white or '00' Italian
   flour, plus extra for dusting
85g (3oz) icing sugar
pinch of salt
115g (4oz) unsalted butter, chilled
1 small egg, beaten
finely grated zest of 1 unwaxed lemon

filling
4 unwaxed lemons
3 eggs
115g (4oz) caster sugar
55g (2oz) ground almonds
150ml (5fl oz) double cream
icing sugar, for dusting

1 To make the pastry, sift the flour, icing sugar and salt into a bowl. Dice the butter, add it to the flour and rub it in until the mixture resembles fine breadcrumbs. Make a well in the centre. Add the beaten egg and lemon zest, and gradually work the flour in from the edges, mixing to a smooth dough. Wrap in greaseproof paper and chill in the fridge for 30 minutes.

2 Preheat the oven to 190°C/375°F/gas mark 5.

3 On a lightly floured surface, roll out the pastry and use it to line a greased 28cm (11in) loose-bottomed flan tin. Do not remove any overhang. With a fork, prick the base all over. Put the tin on a baking tray, line the pastry case with greaseproof paper and weigh down with baking beans. Blind-bake for 15 minutes, until the sides are crisp. Remove the lining and beans and return to the oven for 5 minutes, until the base is crisp. Trim the edges and leave to cool.

4 Reduce the temperature of the oven to 180°C/350°F/gas mark 4.

5 Meanwhile, make the filling. Finely grate the zest of 2 of the lemons and squeeze out the juice from all of the lemons (including the one used for the pastry). In a large bowl, beat the eggs with the caster sugar until the mixture is thick and pale, and leaves a trail when the beaters are lifted. Stir in the lemon zest and juice with the almonds and cream.

6 Pour the filling into the pre-baked pastry case. Bake for 40 minutes, until softly set. Leave until cold, then dust with sifted icing sugar before serving.

Dried peach and lemon tart

This is a fusion of my favourite flavours: dried peaches and delicious, tangy lemons.

1 To make the pastry, sift the flour, icing sugar and salt into a bowl. Dice the butter, add it to the flour and rub it in until the mixture resembles fine breadcrumbs. Make a well in the centre. Add the egg, vanilla extract and lemon zest, and gradually work in the flour from the edges, mixing to form a smooth dough. Wrap in greaseproof paper and chill in the fridge for 30 minutes.

2 Preheat the oven to 190°C/375°F/gas mark 5.

3 On a lightly floured surface, roll out the pastry and use to line a greased 28cm (11in) loose-bottomed flan tin. Roll the rolling pin over the edges of the tin to remove any excess pastry. With a fork, prick the base all over. Line the pastry case with greaseproof paper and weigh down with baking beans. Blind-bake for 15 minutes, until the sides are crisp. Remove the lining and beans and return to the oven for 5 minutes, until the bottom is crisp. Remove from the tin, trim the edges and leave to cool.

4 To make the filling, put the lemon zest and juice, the butter and three-quarters of the sugar in a medium saucepan and heat gently, stirring with a wooden spoon until the butter melts. Stir in the eggs and cook over a medium heat until the mixture thickens and coats the back of the spoon. (Do not allow the mixture to boil or the eggs will curdle.) Remove from the heat and leave to cool.

5 Put the dried peaches and 225ml (8fl oz) water with the remaining sugar in a pan and simmer for about 5 minutes, until soft. Put the peaches into a food processor, add the almond extract and blend to form a purée. Leave to cool.

6 Spread the lemon mixture in the tart case, then add the peach mixture. Cover and chill in the fridge for at least 1 hour before serving. To serve, whip the cream until it holds its shape and pipe on top of the tart. Decorate with mint leaves.

SERVES 10-12

pastry
225g (8oz) plain white or '00' Italian flour, plus extra for dusting
85g (3oz) icing sugar
pinch of salt
115g (4oz) unsalted butter
1 egg, beaten
a few drops of pure vanilla extract
finely grated zest of 1 unwaxed lemon

filling
finely grated zest and juice of 4 unwaxed lemons
115g (4oz) unsalted butter
115g (4oz) caster sugar
4 eggs, lightly beaten
280g (10oz) no-soak dried peaches
1 tsp pure almond extract

to serve
225ml (8fl oz) double cream
a few fresh mint leaves

Pine kernel tart

This tart is enjoyed throughout Italy and many *pasticcerie* will sell a slice with a coffee for breakfast or as an all-day take-away. This particular recipe is the best I know, although there are many regional variations. Please do use fresh pine kernels and store in the fridge to prevent them becoming rancid. There is a huge difference in flavour between Asian and Mediterranean pine kernels – try to find Mediterranean ones if you can.

1 To make the pastry, put the softened butter, caster sugar and egg yolks in a food processor and mix together. Add the flour, lemon zest and salt and mix again. Wrap in greaseproof paper and chill in the fridge for 1 hour.

2 To make the filling, using a wooden spoon, beat the ricotta in a bowl. Add the vanilla extract, double cream, egg yolks, sugar and three-quarters of the pine kernels and mix.

3 Preheat the oven to 190°C/375°F/gas mark 5.

4 On a lightly floured surface, roll out the pastry and use two-thirds to line a greased 20cm (8in) loose-bottomed flan tin. Roll the rolling pin over the edges of the tin to remove any excess pastry. With a fork, prick the base all over. Chill in the fridge for 30 minutes. Line the pastry case with greaseproof paper and weigh down with baking beans. Blind-bake for 20 minutes, until golden. Remove the lining and beans, and trim the edges.

5 Pour the filling into the pastry case. Roll out the remaining pastry and cut into 1cm (½in) strips, the same length as the tart. Use to make a lattice decoration on the tart by laying half the strips at intervals across the surface and the other half across the first layer. Scatter the remaining pine kernels over the top.

6 Bake for 35 minutes, until the pastry is crisp and golden and the filling is firm to the touch. Leave to cool slightly, then serve warm, dusted with sifted icing sugar.

SERVES 8-12

pastry
140g (5oz) unsalted butter, softened
140g (5oz) caster sugar
4 egg yolks
350g (12oz) plain white or '00' Italian
    flour, plus extra for dusting
finely grated zest of 1 unwaxed lemon
pinch of salt

filling
350g (12oz) ricotta
a few drops of pure vanilla extract
50ml (2fl oz) double cream
3 egg yolks
115g (4oz) caster sugar
115g (4oz) pine kernels
icing sugar, for dusting

Grandmother's pie

On a whistle-stop tour of Florence, in search of some interesting breads, I came across this pie and enjoyed a piece for breakfast with an espresso. What a wonderful start to my morning! There are many regional varieties of this dish.

SERVES 15

pastry
450g (1lb) plain white or '00' Italian flour,
    plus extra for dusting
2 tsp baking powder
pinch of salt
225g (8oz) unsalted butter, chilled
175g (6oz) caster sugar
1 tbsp milk
2 tsp pure vanilla extract
1 egg

filling
300ml (10fl oz) milk
115g (4oz) semolina flour
450g (1 lb) ricotta
2 eggs
115g (4oz) granulated sugar
finely grated zest of 2 large unwaxed
    oranges and juice of 1

to serve
4 tbsp apricot conserve
175g (6oz) slivered almonds, toasted
icing sugar, for dusting

1 Preheat the oven to 190°C/375°F/gas mark 5.

2 To make the filling, pour the milk into a medium saucepan, and heat until warm. Stir in the semolina in a thin stream and continue to stir the mixture until it thickens and leaves the sides of the pan. Remove from the heat and leave to cool slightly.

3 In a bowl, mix together the ricotta, eggs, sugar, orange zest and juice. Add the semolina mixture and, using an electric mixer, beat until blended.

4 To make the pastry, sift the flour, baking powder and salt into a bowl. Dice the butter, add it to the flour and rub it in until the mixture resembles fine breadcrumbs. Stir in the sugar. In a small bowl, lightly whisk together the milk, vanilla and egg. Make a well in the centre of the flour mixture. Add the liquids and gradually work in the flour from the edges, mixing to form a smooth dough.

5 Divide the pastry in half. On a lightly floured surface, roll out one-half of the pastry into a 38 x 29cm (15 x 11½in) rectangle. Place the pastry on a greased baking tray. Spread the filling evenly over the pastry to the edges.

6 Roll the remaining pastry into a 38 x 29cm (15 x 11½in) rectangle. Using your rolling pin, carefully lift the pastry and place it over the filling. Using a fork, pinch the edges together.

7 Bake for 30-35 minutes, until golden. While the pie is still warm, brush with apricot conserve and sprinkle with almonds. Leave to cool. Before serving, sprinkle the pie with sifted icing sugar.

Walnut tart

The best walnuts come from the Aosta Valley. When possible, use fresh nuts for their sweetness. In Umbria, where I teach, we grill the walnuts and crack them open especially to make this tart.

1 To make the pastry, beat together the butter and sugar until light and soft. Add the egg yolks one at a time, then mix in the flour. With your hands, bind the mixture together. Wrap in greaseproof paper and chill in the fridge for 30 minutes.

2 Meanwhile, make the filling. Put all the ingredients in a saucepan, bring to the boil and boil for 2 minutes. Remove from the heat and leave to cool.

3 Preheat the oven to 200°C/400°F/gas mark 6.

4 On a lightly floured surface, roll out most of the pastry and use to line a greased 22cm (8½in) loose-bottomed flan tin. Roll the rolling pin over the edges of the tin to remove the excess pastry. Re-roll the trimmings to make a circle for the top.

5 Spread the cooled walnut filling into the case and cover with the pastry top. Using the prongs of a fork, seal the edges together and prick the top.

6 Bake for 30 minutes, until golden. Leave to cool in the tin. Before serving, dust with sifted icing sugar and serve with a dollop of mascarpone.

SERVES 12

pastry
115g (4oz) unsalted butter, softened
55g (2oz) caster sugar
2 egg yolks
225g (8oz) plain white or '00' Italian flour, plus extra for dusting

filling
85g (3oz) caster sugar
1 tsp fresh lemon juice
4 tbsp fragrant honey
225g (8oz) unsalted butter
225g (8oz) chopped walnuts
pinch of salt

to serve
icing sugar
about 200g (7oz) mascarpone, or to taste

Orchard pie

Apples and blackberries are thought of as uniquely British, but the Italians love the combination too, as this lattice pie demonstrates!

SERVES 6

pastry
280g (10oz) plain wholemeal flour, plus extra for dusting
140g (5oz) unsalted butter, chilled
55g (2oz) soft brown sugar
1 egg, separated
a little caster sugar, for dusting

filling
finely grated zest and juice of 1 unwaxed lemon
55g (2oz) soft brown sugar
½ tsp ground cinnamon
1 tbsp semolina
675g (1½lb) cooking apples
225g (8oz) blackberries

1 To make the pastry, put the flour into a bowl. Dice the butter, add it to the flour and rub it in until the mixture resembles fine breadcrumbs. Stir in the sugar, then add the egg yolk and 3 tbsp water, and mix to form a smooth dough. Knead the dough.

2 On a lightly floured surface, roll out the pastry to a rectangle measuring 25 x 10cm (10 x 4in). Fold in 3, then position the pastry so that the folded edges are at the sides. Repeat the rolling and folding twice more. Wrap in greaseproof paper and chill in the fridge for 20 minutes.

3 Preheat the oven to 200°C/400°F/gas mark 6.

4 To make the filling, put the lemon zest, 2 tbsp lemon juice, the sugar, cinnamon and semolina in a bowl, and stir well.

5 Peel, core and chop the apples into large pieces. Stir into the filling mixture with the blackberries.

6 On a lightly floured surface, roll out two-thirds of the pastry and use to line a greased 19cm (7½in) pie plate. Pile the fruit mixture into the dish, then decorate the top with a lattice made from the remaining pastry.

7 Stand the dish on a baking tray and bake for 15 minutes, or until the pastry is tinged with colour. If you wish, remove from the oven, brush with beaten egg white and sprinkle with caster sugar. Bake for a further 25 minutes, covering lightly with foil when well browned. Serve hot.

Jam tart with bitter chocolate sauce

This tart is very easy to do, and the flavours – the sweet jam, with the bitter chocolate – are wonderful.

1 Preheat the oven to 180°C/350°F/gas mark 4.

2 On a lightly floured surface, roll out the pastry and use to line a greased 22cm (8½in) loose-bottomed flan tin. Roll the rolling pin over the edges of the tin to remove any excess pastry. Keep the pastry trimmings.

3 Pour the jam into the pastry case and level it out with a spatula. Cut the remaining pastry into strips and lay across the jam, forming a lattice.

4 Bake for 35-40 minutes. Leave to cool.

5 Toast the nuts for a few minutes in a dry frying pan, then mince them.

6 Break the chocolate into pieces and let it melt in a bain-marie with the cream. Remove from the heat and add the walnut liqueur and the nuts.

7 Take the tart out of the tin, cut it into slices and serve with the warm bitter chocolate sauce.

SERVES 6

200g (7oz) sweet pastry (use any from elsewhere in the chapter)
350g (12oz) apricot jam

sauce
25g (1oz) shelled walnuts
175g (6oz) plain chocolate with 70% cocoa solids
150ml (5fl oz) double cream
1 tbsp walnut liqueur

Chocolate and orange pastries

These small, dome-shaped pastries are made from a very rich sweet pastry dough. This pastry is hard to handle, but it's worth trying, as it melts in the mouth. The shape of these pastries has inspired the Italian name *Minni di Santa Agatha* which, literally translated, means 'breasts of Saint Agatha'.

MAKES ABOUT 12

pastry
225g (8oz) plain white or '00' Italian flour, plus extra for dusting
65g (2½oz) caster sugar
115g (4oz) unsalted butter, softened
1 egg
1 tsp finely grated lemon zest (from an unwaxed lemon)
pinch of salt

filling
1 tbsp shelled hazelnuts, toasted
1 tbsp candied orange peel or mixed peel
25g (1oz) dark chocolate with 50% cocoa solids
225g (8oz) ricotta
55g (2oz) caster sugar
1½ tsp pure vanilla extract
1 egg yolk

to serve
1 egg, beaten
cocoa powder and icing sugar

1 To make the pastry, put the flour and sugar in a food processor and, working on full speed, add the butter in pieces until well mixed. With the food processor still running, add the egg, lemon zest and salt. Turn the pastry out on to greaseproof paper, flatten, cover and chill in the fridge for 30 minutes.

2 For the filling, finely chop the hazelnuts and orange peel, and grate the chocolate. Push the ricotta through a sieve into a bowl. Stir in the sugar, vanilla extract, egg yolk, peel, hazelnuts and chocolate.

3 Remove the pastry from the fridge and allow to come to room temperature. Preheat the oven to 180°C/350°F/gas mark 4.

4 Divide the pastry in half and, on a lightly floured surface, roll out each half to a narrow strip measuring 15 x 56cm (6 x 22in). Arrange heaped teaspoonfuls of the filling in 2 rows along one of the pastry strips, ensuring that there is at least a 2.5cm (1in) space around each spoonful. Brush the pastry between the filling with beaten egg. Carefully place the second strip of pastry on top and press down gently between each mound of filling to seal.

5 Using a plain, round cutter, cut each covered mound of filling to make a circular parcel. Lift each parcel and, with your fingers, gently seal the edges. Place each pastry on a greased baking tray and bake for 15 minutes, until lightly golden. Serve warm, dusted with sifted cocoa powder and icing sugar.

Sicilian filled pastries

These pastries are traditionally made with wooden *cannoli* tubes, which can be bought from specialist kitchen shops. Should these be difficult to find, I have adapted the recipe so that you can make them without the tubes. Alternatively, you can buy ready-made *cannoli* cases from Italian delicatessens.

1 Preheat the oven to 190°C/375°F/gas mark 5. Grease the handles of 2 wooden spoons and line 2 baking trays with baking parchment.

2 To make the *cannoli* pastry cases, melt the butter and leave to cool. Whisk the egg white until stiff, then fold in the sugar. Sift the flour and cocoa powder over the egg mixture and fold in. Trickle the butter around the sides of the bowl and fold in. Put 1 tbsp of the mixture on to each of the prepared baking trays and spread to circles about 10cm (4in) in diameter. Repeat, making 2 circles per baking tray.

3 Bake for 7 minutes, until firm to the touch. Slide a palette knife under each circle, then wrap around the wooden spoons. Leave to cool for 2-3 minutes, then ease off the handles and cool on a wire rack. Use the remaining mixture in the same way to make 8 pastry tubes.

4 To make the filling, put the ricotta into a small bowl and mix in the sugar. Grate the chocolate and fold into the mixture with the nuts, lemon zest, vanilla extract and cinnamon.

5 Fill a piping bag with a large, plain nozzle with the ricotta mixture and use to stuff the pastry tubes.

6 Place the pastries on a serving dish and dust with sifted icing sugar and cocoa powder. Serve at once.

SERVES 8

cannoli pastry
25g (1oz) unsalted butter
1 egg white
55g (2oz) caster sugar
25g (1oz) plain white or '00' Italian flour,
   plus extra for dusting
1 tsp cocoa powder

filling
85g (3oz) ricotta
1 tbsp caster sugar
25g (1oz) dark chocolate with 50%
   cocoa solids
25g (1oz) shelled pistachio nuts, chopped
finely grated zest of ½ unwaxed lemon
½ tsp pure vanilla extract
pinch of ground cinnamon
icing sugar and cocoa powder, for dusting

Chocolate and nut pastries

These little balls are perfectly delicious: hazelnuts, walnuts and chocolate enclosed in a sweet nutty pastry.

SERVES 6

pastry

115g (4oz) plain white or '00' Italian flour

115g (4oz) caster sugar

115g (4oz) unsalted butter, softened
and diced

175g (6oz) shelled hazelnuts and
walnuts, ground

2 tsp pure vanilla extract

pinch of salt

filling

115g (4oz) plain chocolate, chopped into
pieces

200g (7oz) shelled hazelnuts and walnuts

1 To make the pastry, in a bowl mix the flour with the sugar, butter pieces 85g (3oz) of the ground nuts, the vanilla extract and salt, until you get a smooth dough. Put the dough in a bowl, cover and chill in the fridge for 1 hour.

2 Preheat the oven to 180°C/350°F/gas mark 4, and line a baking tray with greaseproof paper.

3 Roll the dough until it is thin and cut it into discs of 5cm (2in) in diameter using a glass or pastry cutter. Re-mix the spare pastry and cut more discs.

4 In the middle of each disc, put a piece of chocolate and a nut, then close the discs up to form small balls. Roll these in the remaining ground nuts to cover them completely.

5 Lay the little balls, seam-side down, on the prepared baking tray and bake for 20 minutes. Serve warm.

Neapolitan ricotta tart

This recipe comes from the Cappuccino Convent at Amalfi. It is rich, and I think it is best eaten the day after it is made.

SERVES 10

pastry
225g (8oz) unsalted butter, softened
175g (6oz) caster sugar
4 egg yolks
450g (1lb) plain white or '00' Italian flour,
  plus extra for dusting

filling
450g (1lb) ricotta
115g (4oz) caster sugar
1 tsp ground cinnamon
finely grated zest and juice of 1
  unwaxed lemon
4 tbsp orange-flower water
115g (4oz) candied orange or mixed peel
1 egg, separated
550ml (scant 1 pint) milk
115g (4oz) vermicelli
a large pinch of salt
icing sugar, for dusting

1 To make the pastry, put the butter and sugar in a bowl and cream together. Add the egg yolks, then gradually add the flour, mixing well to make a soft dough. Wrap in greaseproof paper and chill in the fridge for 30 minutes.

2 To make the filling, put the ricotta, sugar (reserving 2 tbsp), cinnamon, half the lemon zest, the lemon juice, orange-flower water, candied peel and the egg yolk in a bowl and beat together.

3 Preheat the oven to 190°C/375°F/gas mark 5.

4 In a small saucepan bring the milk to the boil and add the vermicelli, the remaining sugar and lemon zest and the salt. Simmer gently until the vermicelli has absorbed all the milk. While still warm, blend the pasta carefully into the ricotta mixture.

5 Whisk the egg white until it just holds its shape, then fold it into the ricotta mixture.

6 On a lightly floured surface, roll out the pastry and use two-thirds to line a greased 28cm (11in) loose-bottomed flan tin. Roll the rolling pin over the edges of the tin to remove any excess pastry. Add the ricotta filling. Cut the remaining pastry into strips and arrange in a lattice on top of the tart.

7 Bake for 40-50 minutes, until golden. Dust with sifted icing sugar before serving warm or cold.

Little jam pastries

This is another typical recipe from Naples. All the pastry shops sell their own variations of this recipe, some of which are filled with jam, while others are filled with custard. I particularly enjoy these for breakfast.

1 To make the pastry cream, cream together the egg and sugar until pale and thick. Sift in the flour and beat until smooth. Heat the cream in a saucepan until almost boiling, then pour on to the egg mixture, stirring all the time. Return to the pan and cook over a low heat, stirring, until it boils and thickens. Remove the pan from the heat and stir in the vanilla extract and lemon zest. Cover the surface with a piece of greaseproof paper and leave to cool completely.

2 Preheat the oven to 200°C/400°F/gas mark 6.

3 To make the pastry, mix together the flour and sugar. Mix in the oil and 6 tbsp water to make a soft dough. On a lightly floured work surface, roll out the pastry and cut into 7.5cm (3in) circles.

4 Place a dab of jam and pastry cream in the centre of each circle. Fold the circle in half and press the edges firmly together to seal. Lay the pastries on a baking tray and brush with the egg yolk.

5 Bake for 12-15 minutes, until golden brown. Leave to cool, then serve dusted with sifted icing sugar.

MAKES 24

pastry
300g (10½oz) plain white or '00' Italian flour, plus extra for dusting
85g (3oz) caster sugar
3 tbsp olive oil

pastry cream
1 egg
1 tbsp caster sugar
1 tbsp plain white or '00' Italian flour
100ml (3½fl oz) single cream
a few drops of pure vanilla extract
finely grated zest of ½ unwaxed lemon

filling and topping
about 2 tbsp blackberry or strawberry jam
1 egg yolk, beaten
icing sugar, for dusting

Ices

Italy is renowned for its *gelati* (ice-creams). It was probably the Arabs who introduced the process of freezing ice and flavourings together, so it's not surprising that Sicily – for so long ruled by the Arabs – has a great repertoire of recipes for ices and related dishes. Ice-creams were first recorded in cookery books in the 17th-century, and they soon spread from Italy through France to the rest of Europe. Here I have included several simple ice-creams that are a combination of flavouring and, usually, double cream. There are also a few water ices or sorbets (which Europe has always been fonder of than the cream ices the British love so much), in which a syrup is used as a base for the principal flavouring. And I've given a recipe for one frozen pudding, the classic biscuit *tortoni*, a delicious amalgam of cream, sugar, nuts, crumbled macaroons and cherries, which is perfect for Christmas.

Biscuit Tortini

'Biscuit Tortoni' is a creation of a Neapolitan ice-cream maker, one Signor Tortoni. Signor Tortoni was to expand his career by moving to Paris, where he opened the famous Café Napolitaine. This delicious dish is popular throughout Italy, especially in Rome.

SERVES 10

300ml (10fl oz) double cream
2 tbsp icing sugar
225g (8oz) chopped almonds, toasted
2 tbsp rum
225g (8oz) amaretti biscuits
10 natural glacé or maraschino cherries,
   or cherries preserved in rum

1 Arrange 10 paper cake cases on a baking tray.

2 Whisk together the cream and icing sugar until stiff. Fold in the almonds and blend in the rum.

3 Break the amaretti biscuits into quarters and put pieces in the bottom of the paper cases. Top each with the cream mixture, then with a cherry.

4 Place in the freezer for 1-2 hours, until firm. Store in the freezer for up to 2 weeks.

5 Transfer to the fridge 45 minutes before serving.

Iced zabaglione

I just couldn't leave this spectacular pudding out of my book. This recipe is one of the simplest to make, and you will never tire of it.

SERVES 4-6

4 egg yolks
115g (4oz) caster sugar
150ml (5fl oz) dry Marsala
150ml (5fl oz) whipping cream

1 Put the egg yolks and sugar into a large, heat-proof bowl and whisk until the mixture is very pale and leaves a trail when the beaters are lifted.

2 Whisk in the Marsala. Stand the bowl over a saucepan of simmering water and continue whisking until the mixture has at least doubled in volume.

3 Remove from the heat, stand the bowl in cold water and whisk until the mixture is cool.

4 Whip the cream until it just holds its shape. Add to the egg mixture and whisk together.

5 Pour the mixture into a freezer container and freeze for about 1½ hours, until firm.

6 Transfer to the fridge 45 minutes before serving. Serve the *zabaglione* in small-stemmed glasses.

Honey ice-cream

Honey ice-cream is a delicious combination of honey, milk and cream. Each year I seem to favour a different honey: at the moment I am enjoying a heather honey, but I have used tilleul (lime) and chestnut honeys.

1 In a bowl, beat the eggs and honey together. Heat the milk in a saucepan until just before boiling, then pour it on to the egg mixture, stirring constantly.

2 Strain the mixture back into the pan and cook over a gentle heat, stirring, until the custard is smooth and coats the back of a wooden spoon. Leave to cool.

3 When cold, whip the cream until stiff, then fold into the custard. Pour into a freezer container and freeze for 3 hours, until frozen. Alternatively, pour the mixture into an ice-cream maker and freeze according to the manufacturer's instructions.

4 Transfer to the fridge 45 minutes before serving.

SERVES 4

3 eggs
3 tbsp fragrant honey
300ml (10fl oz) milk
300ml (10fl oz) double or whipping cream

Chocolate ice-cream

This chapter would not be complete without a recipe for chocolate ice-cream, and this one is for chocolate lovers everywhere. My friend Claudio does not freeze the mixture, but serves it as a delicious mousse.

1 Break the chocolate into a heat-proof bowl and add the milk. Stand the bowl over a saucepan of simmering water and heat until the chocolate has melted. Remove from the heat and leave to cool slightly.

2 Beat the egg yolks into the mixture, one at a time, then add the brandy, if using. Leave to cool.

3 Whip the cream until it holds its shape, then fold into the chocolate mixture. Whisk the egg whites until stiff, then fold these into the mixture too.

4 Pour the mixture into a shallow freezer container and freeze, uncovered, for 2-3 hours until firm. Cover the container with a lid for storing. Transfer to the fridge 45 minutes before serving.

SERVES 4

225g (8oz) dark chocolate with 50% cocoa solids
3 tbsp milk
6 eggs, separated
4 tbsp brandy (optional)
300ml (10fl oz) whipping cream

Italian vanilla ice-cream

This really is an original recipe for Italian ice-cream. It is soft in texture and low in fat because it doesn't contain cream.

SERVES 4-6

700ml (1¼ pints) milk
1 vanilla pod
8 egg yolks
175g (6oz) granulated sugar

1 Pour the milk into a medium saucepan and heat gently until warm. Remove from the heat. Split the vanilla pod lengthways and leave to infuse in the warm milk for 20 minutes.

2 Using an electric whisk, beat together the egg yolks and sugar until very thick. Remove the vanilla pod from the saucepan and scrape the seeds out into the milk. Gradually add the vanilla milk to the egg yolk mixture, stirring.

3 Pour the vanilla custard into an ice-cream machine and freeze according to the manufacturer's instructions. Alternatively, pour into a shallow freezer container and freeze, uncovered, for 1-2 hours, until mushy. Turn the mixture into a bowl and, using a fork, break up the ice crystals. Return to the freezer and repeat, breaking up the ice crystals every 30 minutes for 2 hours.

4 Return to the freezer to become firm. The texture will be softer than you might expect, but this is correct. Cover the container with a lid for storing. Transfer to the fridge 45 minutes before serving.

Fig ice-cream

This recipe uses dried figs, which give the ice-cream a more intense flavour.

SERVES 4

450g (1lb) dried figs, trimmed
115g (4oz) granulated sugar
125ml (4fl oz) water
225ml (8fl oz) milk
125ml (4fl oz) double cream

1 Put the figs and sugar in a food processor and blend until smooth and creamy. Add the water, milk and cream, and blend until well mixed.

2 Pour into an ice-cream machine and freeze according to the manufacturer's instructions. Alternatively, pour into a shallow freezer container and freeze, uncovered, for 1-2 hours, until mushy. Turn the mixture into a bowl and, using a fork, break up the ice crystals. Return to the freezer and repeat, breaking up the ice crystals every 30 minutes for 2 hours.

3 Return to the freezer to become firm. Cover the container with a lid for storing. Transfer to the fridge 45 minutes before serving.

Lemon ice-cream

My love of lemons is well known to everyone close to me, so it's no surprise that this is one of my favourite ice-creams. I hope you enjoy it too.

SERVES 4

thickly pared zest and juice of 3 unwaxed
   lemons
225ml (8fl oz) water
115g (4oz) caster sugar
225ml (8fl oz) double cream

1 Place the pared lemon zest, water and sugar in a saucepan and bring to the boil. Boil for 2 minutes, then remove from the heat and leave to cool. Strain the syrup into a bowl and finely chop the zest. Leave until the syrup is cold.

2 Add the zest, lemon juice and cream to the syrup.

3 Pour into an ice-cream machine and freeze according to the manufacturer's instructions. Alternatively, pour into a shallow freezer container and freeze, uncovered, for 1-2 hours, until mushy. Turn the mixture into a bowl and, using a fork, break up the ice crystals. Return to the freezer and repeat, breaking up the ice crystals every 30 minutes for 2 hours.

4 Return to the freezer to become firm. Cover the container with a lid for storing. Transfer to the fridge 45 minutes before serving.

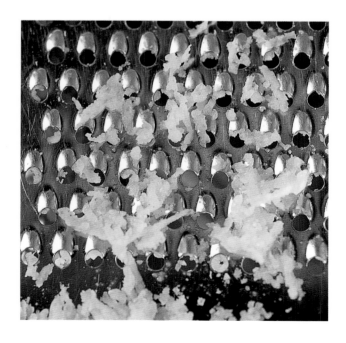

Apricot and lemon sorbet

This combination of fruits is memorable. This recipe is for my mother, a great lover of apricots. Be sure to choose apricots that are fully ripe.

SERVES 6

450g (1lb) ripe apricots
grated zest and juice of 2 unwaxed lemons
115g (4oz) caster sugar

1 Wash and halve the apricots and remove the stones, but do not peel.

2 Put all the ingredients in a food processor and blend until smooth.

3 Pour into an ice-cream machine and freeze according to the manufacturer's instructions. Alternatively, pour into a shallow freezer container and freeze, uncovered, for 1-2 hours, until crystals start to form. Turn the mixture into a bowl and, using a fork, break up the ice crystals. Return to the freezer and repeat, breaking up the ice crystals every 30 minutes for 2 hours.

4 Return to the freezer to become firm. Cover the container with a lid for storing. Transfer to the fridge 45 minutes before serving, in tall glasses.

Lemon water ice

This cool, refreshing Italian classic is enjoyed throughout the country during the blistering hot days of high summer. A variation of this recipe is raspberry and lemon water ice, with the simple addition of 225g (8oz) raspberries. Purée these and add to the cold syrup.

1 Make a sugar syrup by putting the sugar in a saucepan with 450ml (16fl oz) water and heating gently until the sugar dissolves. Bring to the boil, then boil gently for 10 minutes without stirring. Remove from the heat.

2 Meanwhile, using a potato peeler, peel the zest from the lemons and add to the sugar syrup. Leave until cold.

3 Squeeze 450ml (16fl oz) juice from the lemons and pour into a mixing jug. Strain the cold syrup, stir in the lemon juice and mix well.

4 Pour into an ice-cream machine and freeze according to the manufacturer's instructions. Alternatively, pour into a shallow freezer container, cover and freeze for about 40 minutes, until mushy. Turn the mixture into a bowl and, using a fork, break down the ice crystals. Return to the freezer for 40 minutes, until firm.

5 Transfer to the fridge 45 minutes before serving. Spoon into individual glasses and decorate with lemon slices, if wished.

SERVES 6

175g (6oz) granulated sugar
8 large unwaxed lemons
lemon slices, for decorating (optional)

Coffee and cinnamon water ice

This is a classical Italian water ice that is ideal to make when you have some unused espresso coffee.

1 In a jug, add the sugar and cinnamon to the coffee and stir until dissolved. Leave until cold.

2 Pour into an ice-cream machine and freeze according to the manufacturer's instructions. Alternatively, pour the mixture into a shallow freezer container, cover and freeze for about 40 minutes, until just beginning to set. Turn the mixture into a bowl and, using a fork, break up the ice crystals. Return to the freezer for 40 minutes, until firm.

3 Whip the cream with the 2 tsp sugar, until stiff. Transfer to the fridge 45 minutes before serving. To serve, spoon into individual glasses and top with cream.

SERVES 4

85g (3oz) caster sugar, plus 2 tsp
1 tsp freshly ground cinnamon
450ml (16fl oz) hot and strong espresso coffee
225ml (8fl oz) double cream

Orange water ice

There are so many delicious, refreshing water ices in Italy. A *granita* such as this is a water ice that is frozen to a granular texture. It is an exquisite, very cold dessert and perfectly cooling on a hot day.

1 Put all the ingredients in a saucepan and heat gently until the sugar has dissolved, then boil gently for 10 minutes. Leave until cold.

2 Pour into an ice-cream machine and freeze according to the manufacturer's instructions. Alternatively, pour into a shallow freezer container, cover and freeze for about 40 minutes, until crystals start to form. Turn the mixture into a bowl and, using a fork, break up the ice crystals. Return to the freezer for a further 40 minutes, until firm.

3 Transfer to the fridge 45 minutes before serving.

SERVES 4

450ml (16fl oz) freshly squeezed orange juice (about 10 oranges)
juice of 1 unwaxed lemon
3 tbsp granulated sugar

Cakes

Italian cakes are luscious and full of flavour. They are made mainly in *pasticcerie* rather than in restaurants or at home, and most families buy them for special occasions such as Easter or Christmas. These cakes are eaten with coffee in the morning, for *merenda* (at tea time), or after a meal. Chocolate is a favourite cake flavouring in Italy (as it is everywhere), and it is complemented by nuts, such as almonds or hazelnuts. Almonds are a common ingredient too – they grow prolifically in the south – partnered by fruit such as oranges and apples, and by ricotta cheese. Other nuts used in cake-making include pistachios and, perhaps surprisingly, coconut. There is a great Italian tradition of preserving fruit – grapes as raisins, plums as prunes, candied citrus peel – and these wonderful ingredients are included in many cakes. And the Italian sponge cake is as light as the best Victoria, playing an important role in many classic Italian puddings, such as trifle and *cassata*.

Chocolate and rum cake

Rich and delicious, this impressive-looking cake is a specialty of Bologna. My family love to eat it on special occasions, such as birthdays. Always use the very best chocolate – you deserve it!

SERVES 8-10

175g (6oz) dark chocolate with 70% cocoa solids
3 tbsp rum
175g (6oz) unsalted butter, softened
175g (6oz) caster sugar
6 eggs, separated
85g (3oz) self-raising flour
85g (3oz) ground almonds
icing sugar, for dusting

filling
300ml (½ pint) double cream
2 tbsp icing sugar
3 tbsp apricot conserve

chocolate coating
450g (1lb) dark chocolate with 70% cocoa solids

1 Preheat the oven to 180°C/350°F/gas mark 4. Grease and line with baking parchment the base and sides of a 23cm (9in) round, deep cake tin.

2 Break the chocolate into a heat-proof bowl and add the rum. Stand the bowl over a saucepan of simmering water and heat until melted. Remove from the heat and leave to cool slightly.

3 Put the butter and sugar in a bowl and cream together until they are light and fluffy, then gradually beat in the egg yolks. Next beat in the melted chocolate.

4 Whisk the egg whites until stiff, then fold them into the chocolate mixture. Then, using a metal spoon, fold in the flour and almonds. Pour the mixture into the prepared tin and bake for 40-45 minutes, until firm to the touch.

5 Leave to cool in the tin, then turn out on to a wire rack and carefully slice in half horizontally.

6 To make the filling, whip the cream with the icing sugar until it just holds its shape. Use the cream to sandwich the cake halves together. Melt the apricot conserve in a pan, then push it through a sieve. Brush the conserve all over the top of the cake, then place the cake on a large serving plate.

7 To make the chocolate coating, cut a piece of parchment 75 x 6cm (30 x 2½in). Fold under 2.5cm (1in) of the paper at each end of the strip to form handles. Break the chocolate into a heat-proof bowl over a pan of simmering water and heat until melted. Using a brush, cover one side of the parchment paper completely with a fairly thick layer of chocolate. Spread the remaining chocolate on to a cold marble slab.

8 Leave the chocolate strip until it is set but still flexible. Before the chocolate on the marble slab sets, using a large knife, push the blade across the surface of the chocolate to roll pieces off in long curls to form *caraque*. Cover the top of the cake with overlapping curls of chocolate *caraque*. Dust with icing sugar before serving. Lift the chocolate strip by the handles and place around the side of the cake, pressing so that it sticks to the apricot conserve. Carefully peel away the paper.

Chocolate cake

This is one of my all-time favourite recipes, and since I've been making it for so long, I've tended to experiment with it a lot. It was traditionally made at Christmas time, but it is now eaten all year round. To enjoy the cake at its best, eat with a dollop of mascarpone and a cup of strong black coffee. It can be kept for a week, but I doubt that you will be able to resist it for so long.

SERVES 10-12

225g (8oz) dark chocolate with 70%
   cocoa solids
115g (4oz) unsalted butter
5 eggs, separated
140g (5oz) caster sugar
50ml (2fl oz) rum or brandy
100g (3½oz) fine polenta
icing sugar, for dusting

1 Preheat the oven to 180°C/350°F/gas mark 4. Grease and flour a 25cm (10in) loose-bottomed deep, round cake tin.

2 Break the chocolate into a small saucepan, add the butter and heat gently until melted. Remove from the heat.

3 Whisk together the egg yolks and sugar until thick and creamy. Fold in the chocolate mixture, rum and polenta, and mix together well.

4 Whisk the egg whites until stiff but not too dry, then fold them into the chocolate mixture.

5 Pour into the prepared tin and bake for 30-40 minutes, until firm to the touch but still slightly moist. Leave to cool in the tin. The cake will rise, then sink and crack on top, but don't be alarmed.

6 When the cake is cold, turn it out on to a wire rack and dust with sifted icing sugar.

Chocolate and hazelnut cake

I am permanently in pursuit of the perfect chocolate cake, and I am always trying new recipes. This particular cake is dense and dotted with hazelnuts. For extra indulgence, add 2 tbsp of rum with the cocoa powder.

1 Preheat the oven to 180°C/350°F/gas mark 4. Grease and line with parchment paper the base and sides of a 23cm (9in) loose-bottomed round, deep cake tin.

2 In a large bowl and using an electric mixer, cream together the butter and sugar until pale and fluffy. Add 1 egg and the vanilla extract and whisk in well.

3 Sift together the flour, salt, cocoa and baking powder. Using a metal spoon, carefully fold 2 tbsp of the flour mixture into the butter mixture. Continue to add the eggs alternately with the flour mixture to the butter mixture until all the ingredients have been incorporated. Fold in the nuts.

4 Pour the mixture into the prepared tin and bake for 40-50 minutes, until the cake is firm to the touch and coming away from the sides of the tin. Leave to cool in the tin.

5 Before serving, turn the cake out on to a wire rack and dust with sifted icing sugar.

SERVES 8-10

175g (6oz) unsalted butter, softened
115g (4oz) caster sugar
5 eggs
1 tbsp pure vanilla extract
115g (4oz) plain white or '00' Italian flour
½ tsp salt
55g (2oz) cocoa powder
1 tsp baking powder
175g (6oz) chopped hazelnuts, toasted
icing sugar, for dusting

Chocolate and almond cake from Positano

They love their almonds in Positano, and hold festivals in celebration of the annual harvest. The almonds of this area are reputedly the best in Italy, and are used locally in lots of cakes, torrone and other sweet things. This cake is particularly rich and delicious.

SERVES 12

200g (7oz) semi-sweet chocolate with 75% cocoa solids, or more
200g (7oz) unsalted butter
250g (9oz) caster sugar
5 eggs, separated
250g (9oz) blanched almonds, finely chopped
finely grated zest of 1 unwaxed lemon
icing sugar, for dusting

1 Preheat the oven to 190°C/375°F/gas mark 5. Grease and flour a 23cm (9in) loose-bottomed round, deep cake tin.

2 Break the chocolate into a large heat-proof bowl. Stand the bowl over a saucepan of simmering water and heat until the chocolate has melted. Add the butter in pieces and mix until you have a smooth mixture. Add the sugar and mix to a cream consistency. Add the egg yolks and mix together. Remove from the heat and add the almonds.

3 Whisk the egg whites in a bowl until they form peaks. Add the grated lemon zest, then fold gently into the chocolate mixture until blended.

4 Pour the mixture into the prepared tin and bake for 30-45 minutes, or until the cake is golden brown and has pulled away from the sides of the tin.

5 Turn the cake out on to a wire rack, leave to cool and then dust with sifted icing sugar.

Fragrant almond cake

Fresh almonds are my favourite nuts and, used in this recipe, make a wonderfully moist cake. Potato flour is the fine, soft white starch extracted from potatoes after pulverizing and washing. It gives cakes a dry, light texture and is available from health-food shops.

1 Preheat the oven to 180°C/350°F/gas mark 4. Grease and line with baking parchment the base and sides of an 18cm (7in) loose-bottomed deep, round cake tin.

2 Sift the plain flour, potato flour, cinnamon and allspice into a bowl. Add the lemon zest.

3 Add the sugar to the egg yolks in a bowl, and whisk until light and frothy. Fold in the flour mixture, melted butter, almonds and Amaretto.

4 Whisk the egg whites until stiff, then carefully fold into the mixture.

5 Spoon the mixture carefully into the prepared tin, and bake for about 1 hour, until well risen. Turn the cake out on to a rack.

6 Break the chocolate into a heat-proof bowl and add 1 tbsp water. Stand the bowl over a saucepan of simmering water and heat, stirring until the chocolate mixture is melted and smooth. Spread over the cake and leave to set.

SERVES 6

55g (2oz) plain white or '00' Italian flour
55g (2oz) potato flour
pinch of ground cinnamon
pinch of ground allspice
finely grated zest of 1 unwaxed lemon
85g (3oz) caster sugar
4 eggs, separated
40g (1½oz) unsalted butter, melted
55g (2oz) ground almonds
2 tbsp Amaretto
85g (3oz) plain chocolate with 70% cocoa solids

Almond and orange cake

This cake is light, moist and full of flavour. We use a lot of almonds in Italy as they grow so prolifically. The recipe comes from an aunt of mine in Naples.

SERVES 8-10

4 eggs, separated
225g (8oz) granulated sugar
4 tbsp potato flour
350g (12oz) ground almonds
finely grated zest of 3 unwaxed oranges
   and juice of 2
icing sugar, for dusting

1 Preheat the oven to 180°C/350°F/gas mark 4. Grease and flour a 20cm (8in) springform cake tin.

2 Beat together the egg yolks and sugar until pale, thick and creamy. Fold in the potato flour, then fold in the almonds, orange zest and juice.

3 Whisk the egg whites until stiff, then fold into the mixture.

4 Turn into the prepared tin and bake for 45 minutes, until golden brown and firm to the touch.

5 Turn the cake out on to a wire rack, leave to cool and then dust with sifted icing sugar.

Apple, almond and sour cream cake

I love this cake, which is one of those thrown-together recipes, invented to utilize a glut of apples and whatever I had in the fridge – in this case some soured cream.

1 Preheat the oven to 180°C/350°F/gas mark 4. Grease and line with baking parchment the base and sides of a 20cm (8in) deep sandwich tin, then sprinkle with the demerara sugar.

2 Cream together the butter and sugar until light and fluffy. Beat in the egg yolks and vanilla extract, then fold in the almonds, flour and soured cream.

3 Whisk the egg whites until they hold their shape and then, using a metal spoon, fold them into the creamed mixture.

4 Peel, core and slice the apples and arrange in the base of the prepared tin.

5 Spoon the creamed mixture over the apples and level the surface. Bake for 45 minutes to 1 hour, until golden and firm to the touch.

6 Serve cold or warm with the whipped cream.

SERVES 4-6

1 tbsp demerara sugar
115g (4oz) unsalted butter, softened
115g (4oz) caster sugar
2 eggs, separated
2 drops pure vanilla extract
115g (4oz) ground almonds
55g (2oz) self-raising flour
150ml (5fl oz) soured cream
175g (6oz) Cox's Orange Pippin or
   Braeburn apples
whipped cream, to serve

Ricotta cake with almond cream

A gorgeous cake, made with one of Italy's most delicious soft cheeses, served with a sumptuous almond custard-like sauce.

SERVES 6

280g (10oz) ricotta
3 tbsp double cream
finely grated zest of 1 unwaxed lemon
3 eggs, separated
115g (4oz) caster sugar
10g (¼oz) fresh yeast
225g (8oz) plain white or '00' Italian flour
grated zest of 1 unwaxed lemon, to
    decorate (optional)

almond cream
400ml (14fl oz) milk
1 clove
2 peppercorns
4 egg yolks
125g (4½oz) caster sugar
75g (2¾oz) ground almonds
a drop of pure vanilla extract

1 Preheat the oven to 190°C/375°F/gas mark 5. Grease and flour a 23cm (9in) springform cake tin.

2 Mix the ricotta with the cream, lemon zest, egg yolks and sugar.

3 Whisk the egg whites in a bowl until they form stiff peaks.

4 Combine the yeast with 2 tbsp hand-hot water. Mix the flour with the yeast water in a large bowl. Pour in the ricotta mixture, stirring well with a wooden spoon. Fold in the whisked egg whites. Pour the mixture into the prepared tin and bake for 45 minutes.

5 Meanwhile, make the almond cream. Bring the milk to the boil with the clove and peppercorns, then strain, cover and leave to cool a little. Whisk the egg yolks with the sugar, add the almonds and vanilla, then, gradually, add the strained milk. Stir well, then cook, whisking continuously to avoid lumps forming, until the creamy custard-like sauce falls from the spoon. Leave aside until lukewarm.

6 Turn the cake out on to a wire rack and leave to cool. Serve with a dollop of the almond cream. You can decorate with grated lemon zest if you wish.

Pistachio cake

Other nuts can be substituted in this sumptuous yet simple cake from Sicily. Walnuts work well. It is a very rich cake and you can dust with icing sugar instead of topping with cream, if you prefer.

1 Preheat the oven to 180°C/350°F/gas mark 4. Grease and line with baking parchment the base and sides of a 23cm (9in) loose-bottomed round, deep cake tin.

2 Beat together the egg yolks and half of the sugar until thick and creamy. Sift together the flour, baking powder and salt, then stir into the egg yolk mixture. Gradually beat in the remaining sugar. Fold in the nuts.

3 Whisk the egg whites until stiff, then fold into the mixture.

4 Pour the mixture into the prepared tin and bake for about 45 minutes, until well risen, golden and firm to the touch.

5 Turn the cake out on to a wire rack and leave to cool. Before serving, whisk the cream until stiff. Spread it on top of the cake and decorate with the whole pistachio nuts.

SERVES 10-12

6 eggs, separated
250g (9oz) granulated sugar
2 tbsp plain white or '00' Italian flour
2 tsp baking powder
½ tsp salt
350g (12oz) shelled pistachios, finely chopped, plus extra whole pistachios, for decorating
300ml (10fl oz) double cream

Blackberry and cinnamon cake

This is crumbly and succulent with blackberries, but you can use other berries as an alternative. This cake is full of childhood memories for me. It is particularly good served with mascarpone and strong black coffee.

SERVES 8-12

140g (5oz) unsalted butter, softened
140g (5oz) caster sugar
140g (5oz) ground almonds
140g (5oz) self-raising flour
1 egg
2 tsp ground cinnamon
2 tsp pure vanilla extract
225g (8oz) fresh blackberries
icing sugar, for dusting

1 Preheat the oven to 180°C/ 350°F/gas mark 4. Grease and line with baking paper the base of a 23cm (9in) springform tin.

2 Put the butter, sugar, almonds, flour, egg, half the cinnamon and the vanilla extract into a bowl and beat well together.

3 Put half the mixture in the prepared tin and, using a fork, flatten lightly. Sprinkle over the blackberries and dot over the remaining almond mixture so that it covers the fruit.

4 Put the tin on a baking tray and bake for 1 hour, until golden on top but springy. Leave to cool in the tin.

5 Turn the cake out on to a wire rack and dust the top with the remaining cinnamon and some icing sugar, sifted.

Farmhouse apple cake

I've written many apple cake recipes, but this one is our family favourite. It is very quick to prepare, and has a moist pudding texture. Serve a thin wedge with either a dollop of cream or vanilla or honey ice-cream (see pages 88 and 85).

SERVES 8

5 Golden Delicious apples
2 eggs
225g (8oz) caster sugar
55g (2oz) plain white or '00' Italian flour
125ml (4fl oz) whole milk
100g (3½oz) unsalted butter, melted
   and cooled
1 tsp pure vanilla extract
2 tsp baking powder
icing sugar, for dusting

1 Preheat the oven to 190°C/375°F/gas mark 5. Grease and flour a 28cm (11in) loose-bottomed round cake tin or deep-dish pizza pan.

2 Peel, core and quarter the apples. Slice the apple sections crosswise into very thin slivers.

3 Beat the eggs and sugar together in a large bowl with a wire whisk until the sugar has dissolved. Sift and stir in the flour, then mix in the milk, melted butter and vanilla. Blend the mixture thoroughly. Quickly stir in the baking powder, then fold in the sliced apples.

4 Pour the mixture into the prepared tin and bake on the floor of the oven for 10 minutes. Transfer the tin to the centre rack and bake for a further 50-55 minutes, until the cake is golden brown.

5 Turn the cake out on to a wire cooling rack and leave to cool. Serve warm or at room temperature, dusted with sifted icing sugar.

Rosie's cake

Rosie is a friend of mine, who was brought up in a small Italian community in Africa. We love talking about food and Rosie recently made this wonderful cake for me. I just couldn't stop eating it.

1 Preheat the oven to 180°C/350°F/gas mark 4. Grease and line with baking paper the base and sides of a deep 25cm (10in) loose-bottomed round, deep cake tin.

2 Peel, core and slice the apples. Put them into a bowl, pour over the wine and leave for 20 minutes.

3 Whisk together the eggs and sugar until thick and creamy. Gradually whisk in the oil and vanilla extract. Fold in the flour, 1 tbsp at a time and, finally, add the apple and wine mixture and the cinnamon. Stir gently until mixed.

4 Pour the mixture into the prepared tin and bake for 1 hour, until firm to the touch.

5 Meanwhile, prepare the topping. Roughly chop the almonds and mix together with the sugar and cinnamon. Sprinkle over the top of the cake as soon as it is cooked. Turn the cake out on to a wire rack and leave to cool.

SERVES 8-10

4 Cox's orange pippin apples
150ml (5fl oz) sweet red wine
3 eggs
115g (4oz) caster sugar
150ml (5fl oz) sunflower oil
1 tbsp pure vanilla extract
225g (8oz) self-raising flour
1 tbsp ground cinnamon

topping
55g (2oz) whole blanched almonds
55g (2oz) caster sugar
1 tbsp ground cinnamon

Carrot cake

This recipe has been given to me by Antonietta Balducci, a great friend of mine from Umbria. She has just opened her own *pasticceria* in the village of Selci Lama. It is a moist cake that is best eaten on the day it is made.

SERVES 12

5 eggs, separated
200g (7oz) caster sugar
300g (10½oz) carrots, peeled and grated
250g (9oz) ground hazelnuts
2 tsp pure vanilla extract
85g (3oz) fresh breadcrumbs
½ tsp baking powder
finely grated zest of 1 unwaxed lemon
1 tbsp rum
½ tsp ground cinnamon
pinch of salt
icing sugar, for dusting

1 Preheat the oven to 170°C/325°F/gas mark 3. Grease and line with baking parchment the base and sides of a 25cm (10in) loose-bottomed round, deep cake tin.

2 Put the egg yolks and sugar in a heat-proof bowl standing over a saucepan of gently simmering water. Whisk for 10-15 minutes, until the mixture is thick and creamy. Remove from the heat and fold in the grated carrot, ground hazelnuts, vanilla, breadcrumbs, baking powder, lemon zest, rum, cinnamon and salt.

3 Whisk the egg whites until stiff, then carefully fold them into the mixture.

4 Pour the mixture into the prepared tin and bake for 1 hour, until firm to the touch.

5 Turn the cake out on to a wire rack and leave to cool. Serve dusted with sifted icing sugar.

Coconut cake

An unusual nut flavouring for Italy, but a recipe that my aunt in Naples swears by – justifiably, as it is delicious!

1 Preheat the oven to 180°C/350°F/gas mark 4. Grease and flour a 20cm (8in) loose-bottomed cake tin.

2 Grind the nuts in a food processor with 2 tbsp of the sugar.

3 Break the chocolate into a heat-proof bowl and add the butter. Stand the bowl over a saucepan of simmering water until the mixture is smooth, then leave to cool. Add the vanilla.

4 Using a hand-held electric whisk, beat the egg yolks and 85g (3oz) of the sugar together until creamy and light. Add the chocolate mixture.

5 Add the salt to the flour and mix with the ground nuts and coconut. Add the dry ingredients to the chocolate mixture.

6 Whisk the egg whites with the baking powder until stiff, then add the remaining sugar.

7 Add 1 tbsp of the whipped egg white to the chocolate mixture, and stir in to loosen. Fold in the remainder carefully.

8 Pour into the cake tin and bake for 20 minutes. You want the cake to stay fairly soft in the middle.

9 Let the cake cool in the tin. Run a knife around the sides of the cake and invert it on to a serving plate.

SERVES 6

85g (3oz) shelled hazelnuts
140g (5oz) caster sugar
175g (6oz) plain chocolate with 70% cocoa solids
175g (6oz) unsalted butter
2 tsp pure vanilla extract
4 eggs, separated
pinch of salt
55g (2oz) plain white or '00' Italian flour
85g (3oz) desiccated coconut
pinch of baking powder

Harvest grape cake

I first enjoyed this cake during a long weekend trip to see friends in Verona. It should be made when black grapes are at their best, after the harvest at the end of September or early October.

1 Preheat the oven to 180°C/350°F/gas mark 4. Grease and flour a 20cm (8in) loose-bottomed round, deep cake tin.

2 Dust the grapes with a little flour.

3 Put the flour, sugar and baking powder in a large bowl. Add the eggs, one at a time, beating well after each addition, until the mixture is the consistency of batter. Add the grapes and olive oil, and mix well together.

4 Pour the mixture into the prepared tin and bake for 45 minutes, until golden and well risen. Turn the cake out on to a wire rack and leave to cool.

5 When cold, dust the top with sifted icing sugar, if liked.

SERVES 6-8

450g (1lb) seedless sweet black grapes
225g (8oz) plain white or '00' Italian flour
140g (5oz) golden caster sugar
1½ tsp baking powder
5 eggs
3 tbsp olive oil
icing sugar, for dusting (optional)

Orange ring cake

This recipe comes from Florence and is very popular with children. The cake keeps well in an airtight tin.

SERVES 6-8

140g (5oz) unsalted butter
2 eggs, separated
100ml (3½fl oz) milk
200g (7oz) caster sugar
finely grated zest of 2 unwaxed oranges
200g (7oz) plain white or '00' Italian flour
1 tsp baking powder
icing sugar, for dusting

1 Preheat the oven to 180°C/350°F/gas mark 4. Grease and flour a 1.7 litre (3 pint) ring mould.

2 Melt the butter and set aside to cool.

3 Whisk the egg whites until stiff. Add the egg yolks, milk, sugar and orange zest, and fold in for 1-2 minutes.

4 Sift the flour and baking powder into a bowl and, using a metal spoon, fold in alternately with the melted butter.

5 Spoon the mixture into the prepared tin and bake for about 30 minutes, until golden and firm to the touch.

6 Leave the cake in the tin for about 5 minutes, then turn it out on to a wire rack and leave to cool. Before serving, dust with sifted icing sugar.

Paradise cake

My grandparents' home in Italy is called Torre Paradiso, which means 'paradise castle'. The house is actually part of a terrace, close to and part of a castellated fortification. It is a most unusual location. This is a classical *nonna* or 'grandmother' cake, found throughout the length and breadth of Italy. We use the cake for celebrations, split into three, soaked with liqueur or coffee, and filled with cream and fruit.

1 Preheat the oven to 170°C/325°F/gas mark 3. Grease and flour a 25cm (10in) springform cake tin and sprinkle the surface with breadcrumbs. Turn the tin upside down and tap out all the excess crumbs.

2 Dice the butter and put it in a bowl. Add the sugar and mix together with an electric whisk until blended, light and fluffy. Add an egg at a time, beating constantly. Do not add another egg until the previous one is totally incorporated.

3 Sift the potato flour with the cream of tartar, bicarbonate of soda and salt, and sprinkle large spoonfuls over the surface of the butter cream. Fold each spoonful of flour in with a large metal spoon. Mix in the lemon zest.

4 Spoon the mixture into the prepared tin and bake for 45 minutes, until golden brown. Turn out the cake and leave to cool on a wire rack.

5 We often eat this cake with just icing sugar dusted on top, or it can be split and filled with various fillings (see introduction).

SERVES 6-8

fine dried breadcrumbs, to line the tin
325g (11½oz) unsalted butter, softened
325g (11½oz) caster sugar
4 eggs
325g (11½oz) potato flour
½ tsp cream of tartar
½ tsp bicarbonate of soda
½ tsp salt
finely grated zest of 2 unwaxed lemons
icing sugar, for dusting

Lemon polenta cake

There are many variations of this cake – I do hope you will like mine. I serve it with a spoonful of mascarpone and some coffee.

SERVES 8-12

280g (10oz) unsalted butter, softened
225g (8oz) caster sugar
6 eggs, separated
175g (6oz) ground almonds
115g (4oz) coarse polenta
finely grated zest and juice of 4 unwaxed lemons
icing sugar, for dusting

1 Preheat the oven to 180°C/350°F/gas mark 4. Grease and line with baking parchment the base and sides of a 25cm (10in) loose-bottomed round, deep cake tin.

2 Cream the butter and sugar together until thick and creamy. Add the egg yolks, one at a time, beating between each addition.

3 Add the almonds, polenta, lemon zest and juice to the mixture, and mix well.

4 Whisk the egg whites until stiff. Using a metal spoon, fold into the mixture.

5 Pour the mixture into the prepared tin and bake for about 50 minutes, until golden and firm to the touch. Leave to cool in the tin.

6 Turn the cake out on to a wire rack and dust with sifted icing sugar.

Strawberry and pistachio cake

This is truly delicious and it will win you many gasps of approval as it looks so stunning. Make it when strawberries are at their best, in the summer.

1 Preheat the oven to 180°C/350°F/gas mark 4. Grease and line with baking parchment 2 x 20cm (8in) round sandwich tins.

2 Melt the butter in a small saucepan and leave to cool.

3 Put the eggs, sugar and vanilla extract in a bowl. Whisk until pale and thick enough to leave a ribbon-like trail for 8 seconds when the whisk is lifted.

4 Sift the flour and fold half of it into the egg mixture. Pour a little of the cooled butter around the edge of the mixture and carefully fold in 2 tbsp of the remaining flour. Repeat, folding carefully to ensure you maintain a mousse-like consistency, until all the butter and flour is used up. Divide the mixture in half and spoon one-half into one of the prepared tins. Fold 25g (1oz) of the pistachio nuts into the remaining mixture and pour into the other tin.

5 Bake both cakes for 35-40 minutes, or until they have just started shrinking from the sides of the tin. Cool in the tins for 5 minutes. Turn the cakes out on to a wire rack and leave to cool.

6 To fill and decorate, thinly slice the strawberries. Sprinkle the Marsala over the plain cake and then split both cakes in half horizontally. Whip the cream until it just holds its shape and divide into 2 portions. Set one portion aside.

7 Place a pistachio cake layer on a flat plate and spread over half of one portion of the cream. Add a plain cake layer, half the strawberries, another pistachio cake layer and the remaining cream. Top with the plain cake layer.

8 Coat the top and sides of the cake with two-thirds of the reserved cream. Lightly press the remaining pistachio nuts on the sides of the cake. Spoon the remaining cream in blobs around the top of the cake and decorate with the remaining strawberries.

SERVES 8-12

55g (2oz) unsalted butter
100g (3½oz) shelled and skinned pistachio
  nuts, ground
6 eggs, beaten
140g (5oz) caster sugar
a few drops of pure vanilla extract
140g (5oz) plain white or '00' Italian flour

filling and decoration
350g (12oz) fresh strawberries, plus a few
  to decorate
1 tbsp Marsala
600ml (1 pint) double cream

Bolognese Christmas cake

This is the cake made in Bologna at Christmas, and very 'special' it is too. The recipe was created by the monks of Certosa, who made it for the Cardinal Lambertini. Like British Christmas cakes, it should be made in advance, about a month.

1   Soak the raisins in the Marsala for at least 30 minutes, preferably overnight.

2   Preheat the oven to 180°C/350°F/gas mark 4. Grease and line the base and sides of a 23cm (9in) loose-bottomed round, deep cake tin.

3   Heat together the honey, sugar, butter and 2 tbsp water until the sugar dissolves. Crush the fennel seed or aniseed and add to the mixture along with the cinnamon. Pour into a large bowl.

4   Coarsely chop the chocolate. Peel, core and grate the apples, and chop the orange peel. Add the raisins, chocolate, apples, orange peel, flour, almonds, pine kernels and baking powder to the bowl, and mix well together.

5   Pour the mixture into the prepared tin and bake for about 1¾ hours, or until a skewer inserted in the centre comes out clean. Leave to cool in the tin for 15 minutes before turning out on to a wire rack and leaving to cool completely.

6   Wrap in parchment paper and then foil and store for a month before eating.

7   After a month, or before Christmas, brush with two-thirds of the jam, stud with the crystallized fruit and almonds, then brush with the remaining jam.

SERVES 16

250g (9oz) raisins
3 tbsp Marsala
5 tbsp fragrant honey
225g (8oz) caster sugar
85g (3oz) unsalted butter
1 tbsp fennel seed or aniseed
1 tbsp ground cinnamon
115g (4oz) dark chocolate with 50%
   cocoa solids
6 eating apples
115g (4oz) candied orange peel
500g (1lb 2oz) plain white or '00'
   Italian flour
225g (8oz) blanched almonds, coarsely
   chopped
115g (4oz) pine kernels
½ tsp baking powder

to finish
3 tbsp apricot jam
crystallized fruit
blanched toasted almonds

Fruit cake ring

I have enjoyed this in Bar Sandi in Perugia, where I take my students for coffee and cake. I've always arrived when it's been too busy to ask for the recipe, so this is my own version.

1 Preheat the oven to 200°C/400°F/gas mark 6. Grease and flour a 20cm (8in) ring or savarin mould.

2 Chop the figs and apricots into small pieces.

3 Put the butter and sugar in a bowl and cream together until pale and fluffy. Add the egg yolks and mix well. Sift the flour and cinnamon, and fold into the creamed mixture. Add the figs, apricots, raisins and lemon zest, and mix well.

4 Whisk the egg whites until stiff. Using a metal spoon, fold them into the creamed mixture.

5 Spoon into the prepared tin and bake for 30 minutes, until a skewer inserted into the centre comes out clean.

6 Turn out on to a wire rack and leave to cool. When cold, dust with sifted icing sugar.

SERVES 8

85g (3oz) dried figs
85g (3oz) dried apricots, preferably unsulphured
225g (8oz) unsalted butter, softened
200g (7oz) caster sugar
4 eggs, separated
225g (8oz) plain white or '00' Italian flour
1 tbsp ground cinnamon
55g (2oz) raisins
finely grated zest of 1 unwaxed lemon
icing sugar, for dusting

Rum cake

This is my favourite variation of a classical Italian cake. It is best eaten on the day it is made, accompanied by an espresso coffee.

SERVES 12

200g (7oz) unsalted butter
6 eggs
200g (7oz) caster sugar
225g (8oz) plain white or '00' Italian flour
1 tsp pure vanilla extract
4 tbsp dark rum

rum butter frosting
115g (4oz) unsalted butter, softened
225g (8oz) icing sugar
1 egg, beaten
1 tsp pure vanilla extract
2 tbsp dark rum

1 Preheat the oven to 180°C/350°F/gas mark 4. Grease and flour a 23cm (9in) loose-bottomed round, deep cake tin.

2 Melt the butter and set aside to cool. Put the eggs and sugar in a heat-proof bowl standing over a saucepan of gently simmering water. Whisk until the mixture is thick, pale and tripled in volume.

3 Remove the bowl from the heat and gradually fold in the flour. Slowly trickle the melted butter around the edge of the bowl, then fold that in with the vanilla extract.

4 Pour the mixture into the prepared tin and bake for 30-35 minutes, until golden brown and firm to the touch. Turn the cake out on to a wire rack and leave to cool.

5 Cut the cake in half horizontally, and sprinkle each half with the rum.

6 To make the frosting, cream the butter until it is soft and fluffy. Gradually beat in some of the icing sugar. Beat in the egg, vanilla extract and rum. Gradually beat in the remaining sugar.

7 When the cake has cooled completely, spread about half of the frosting over one layer and put the second layer on top. Spread the frosting over the second layer, then over the sides of the cake. Chill the cake in the fridge to harden the frosting and make it easier to slice.

Spiced honey cake

I love honey that is rich and fragrant. In Italy we have so many
varieties, such as chestnut, rosemary, sunflower, lavender and
lemon blossom. This is a moist cake, best eaten the day after
it is made.

1 Preheat the oven to 170°C/325°F/gas mark 3. Grease and line with baking
parchment a 28 x 23cm (11 x 9in) roasting tin.

2 Sift the flour and spices into a large bowl. Put the butter, sugar and honey
in a saucepan and heat gently until the ingredients become runny. Remove
from the heat and leave to cool.

3 Crack the eggs into a measuring jug and make up to 300ml (10fl oz) with
milk. Whisk together.

4 Pour the melted mixture into the sifted dry ingredients and add the egg
and milk mixture. Using a balloon whisk, blend the ingredients together.

5 Pour the batter into the prepared tin and bake for about 1 hour, until a
skewer inserted in the centre comes out clean. (Do not touch the surface –
it's hot!). Leave to cool in the tin.

MAKES 12 SQUARES

225g (8oz) self-raising flour
1 tsp ground cinnamon
½ tsp freshly grated nutmeg
¼ tsp ground mixed spice
85g (3oz) unsalted butter
115g (4oz) soft brown sugar
175g (6oz) your favourite honey
2 eggs
about 175ml (6fl oz) milk

Genoese sponge cake

This light sponge is ideal to use as the base for all Italian gâteaux. It can be simply filled with cream or another filling of your choice.

SERVES 8-10

55g (2oz) unsalted butter
4 eggs
115g (4oz) caster sugar
pinch of salt
115g (4oz) plain white or '00' Italian flour

1 Preheat the oven to 180°C/350°F/gas mark 4. Grease and line with baking parchment the base and sides of a 23cm (9in) round, deep cake tin.

2 Melt the butter, then set aside to cool.

3 Put the eggs, sugar and salt in a heat-proof bowl, standing over a saucepan of gently simmering water. Whisk until the mixture is thick, pale and tripled in volume. Remove the bowl from the heat and continue to whisk until the mixture is cool.

4 Sift some of the flour over the top of the mixture. Slowly trickle in some of the cooled, melted butter around the edge of the bowl then, using a metal spoon, gently fold in both ingredients. Repeat until all the flour and butter are used up. It is essential you maintain a mousse-like consistency.

5 Pour the mixture into the prepared tin and bake for 25-30 minutes, until golden brown, firm to the touch and shrunk slightly from the sides of the tin. Leave to cool in the tin for 1-2 minutes, then turn out on to a wire rack to cool completely.

Italian sponge cake

This cake came to Italy via the Spanish invaders of the island of Sicily. Although Spanish in origin, the cake is so popular in Italy that I can happily call it 'Italian sponge cake'! It can be eaten by itself, of course, but it is very good for using in trifles.

1   Preheat the oven to 180°C/350°F/gas mark 4. Grease and flour a 23cm (9in) loose-bottomed, round, deep cake tin.

2   Whisk together the egg yolks and sugar until thick and creamy.

3   Whisk the egg whites until stiff, then gently fold into the egg mixture. Gradually sift in and fold in the flour. Add the lemon zest, vanilla and rum, and mix together until well blended.

4   Pour the mixture into the prepared tin and bake for 30-35 minutes, until golden brown and well risen. Turn out on to a wire rack and leave to cool.

SERVES 12

5 eggs, separated
225g (8oz) caster sugar
200g (7oz) plain white or '00' Italian flour
finely grated zest of 2 unwaxed lemons
1 tsp pure vanilla extract
1 tsp rum

Biscuits

The Italians love biscuits. They bake them or buy them for everyday eating or for special occasions such as Christmas, All Saints' Day (1 November) and All Souls' Day (2 November). There is a great variety of tastes in the different regions of Italy. However, most Italian biscuits use many of the same ingredients as Italian cakes and puddings – almonds, fruit and chocolate, for instance – and many, particularly those eaten at festive times such as Christmas, have added spices. Italian biscuits are generally crisp, and can be eaten to accompany a creamy pud or ice-cream, or dunked into a glass of Vin Santo after a meal. Many biscuits can be used as part of another sweet offering: *savoiardi* (Italian lady's sponge fingers), for instance, form the base of trifle and *cassata*, and amaretti biscuits are crumbled to make a delicious stuffing for baked peaches.

Florentines

These are ideal for sharing with friends who pop round for coffee, and they make good presents if wrapped attractively.

MAKES 12

115g (4oz) whole blanched almonds
115g (4oz) whole blanched hazelnuts
115g (4oz) shelled Brazil nuts
225g (8oz) natural glacé cherries
115g (4oz) glacé fruits such as melon,
    pineapple, papaya, orange and lemon
55g (2oz) plain white or '00' Italian flour
½ tsp ground allspice
½ tsp freshly grated nutmeg
115g (4oz) caster sugar
115g (4oz) honey
55g (2oz) plain chocolate with 70%
    cocoa solids

1 Preheat the oven to 180°C/350°F/gas mark 4. Grease a 23cm (9in) round cake tin, and line with baking parchment.

2 Put the almonds, hazelnuts and Brazil nuts on a baking tray and roast for 8-10 minutes. Put in a mixing bowl and cool. Wash and dry the cherries and glacé fruits, and add to the nuts.

3 Sift the flour, ground allspice and nutmeg over the glacé fruits and nuts, and mix well.

4 In a saucepan, warm the sugar and honey together over a low heat until the sugar has dissolved. Add the honey mixture to the fruit, and stir.

5 Turn the mixture into the prepared tin and level the top. Bake for 25-30 minutes. Leave to cool in the tin.

6 Break the chocolate into small pieces and melt in a pan over boiling water. Spread over the nut mixture in an even layer. When cold, cut into wedges and serve.

Spiced Christmas biscuits

These delicious cookies can be enjoyed throughout the year and are good served with fresh coffee, Vin Santo or ice-cream. I serve these to my newly arrived students at the cookery school in Umbria. They disappear quickly.

MAKES 28

115g (4oz) amaretti biscuits
25g (1oz) dried figs
65g (2½oz) caster sugar
55g (2oz) white or '00' Italian flour
25g (1oz) ground almonds
dash of pure vanilla extract
finely grated zest of ½ unwaxed lemon
½ tsp baking powder
½ tsp ground cinnamon
25g (1oz) sultanas
1 egg white
1 tbsp dry white wine
icing sugar, for sprinkling

1 Preheat the oven to 180°C/350°F/gas mark 4. Grease several large baking trays.

2 Finely grind the amaretti biscuits and chop the figs. Put in a bowl with all the remaining ingredients except the egg white, wine and icing sugar. Make a well in the centre, add the egg white and wine, and mix to form stiff dough. On a lightly floured surface, knead vigorously for about 10 minutes. The dough will become stickier when kneaded.

3 Shape the dough into flat cookies, the size of chestnuts, and place on the prepared baking trays. Bake for 18-20 minutes, until dry and the surface is slightly cracked. Transfer to a wire rack and leave to cool.

4 Sprinkle with sifted icing sugar before serving. Store in an air-tight tin.

Orange and almond spice cookies

This recipe has proved immensely popular with my friends. *Baci di dama*, the Italian name for these cookies, actually means 'lady's kisses'.

1 Preheat the oven to 180°C/350°F/gas mark 4. Line several baking trays with parchment paper.

2 Very finely chop the orange peel and put in a bowl. Add the almonds and sugar and sift in the flour, reserving 1 tbsp, and mixed spice. Mix well together, then add enough milk to form a smooth, firm dough.

3 Roll the mixture into 24 small balls and place, well apart, on the baking trays. Sprinkle with the remaining flour.

4 Bake for 15 minutes, until golden brown. Transfer to a wire rack and leave to cool.

5 Break the chocolate into pieces and melt in a bowl over a pan of simmering water. Use a little to sandwich the cookies together in pairs.

MAKES 12

115g (4oz) candied orange peel
115g (4oz) ground almonds
115g (4oz) caster sugar
115g (4oz) plain white or '00' Italian flour
½ tsp mixed spice
about 6 tbsp milk
55g (2oz) dark chocolate with 70% cocoa solids

Garibaldi biscuits

These are eaten all over Italy. They are blissfully straightforward to make and children love them.

1 Preheat the oven to 180°C/350°F/gas mark 4. Lightly grease a 30 x 20cm (12 x 8in) Swiss roll tin.

2 Sift the flour into a mixing bowl. Dice and rub in the butter until it is evenly distributed and the mixture resembles fine breadcrumbs. Stir in the sugar and currants.

3 Add almost all the beaten egg to bind the ingredients together, and form a soft but not sticky dough.

4 Turn the dough into the prepared tin and roll it out so that the base is evenly covered and the surface is smooth. Brush the remaining egg over the dough and sprinkle the top with the extra caster sugar.

5 Bake for about 20 minutes, until golden brown. As soon as the pastries are cooked, cut them into 24 rectangles. Transfer to a wire rack and leave to cool.

MAKES 24

115g (4oz) plain white or '00' Italian flour
85g (3oz) unsalted butter, chilled
55g (2oz) caster sugar, plus a little extra
  to finish
115g (4oz) currants
1 egg, beaten

Almond curls

These biscuits are real favourites served with Italian vanilla ice-cream – or any other ice-cream for that matter!

MAKES 18

140g (5oz) ground almonds
85g (3oz) caster sugar
pinch of ground cinnamon
finely grated zest of ½ unwaxed lemon
2 egg whites

1 Preheat the oven to 180°C/350°F/gas mark 4. Grease and line several baking trays with baking parchment.

2 Mix together the almonds, sugar, cinnamon and lemon zest.

3 Whisk the egg whites until stiff, then fold into the almond mixture.

4 Put the mixture in a piping bag fitted with a large nozzle and pipe out on to the baking trays in an S shape, 5cm (2in) long. Allow plenty of space for spreading.

5 Bake for 10 minutes, until golden. Transfer to a wire rack and leave to cool.

Almond crumble cake

This is an old recipe from northern Italy and, although the result is not dissimilar to shortbread, in Italy it is considered a cake to be served on feast days. It is really a cross between a biscuit and a cake.

1 Preheat the oven to 170°C/325°F/gas mark 3. Grease a 23cm (9in) round cake tin.

2 Put the flour and cornmeal into a bowl. Dice and rub in the butter until the mixture resembles breadcrumbs.

3 Stir in the almonds and sugar, then add the egg yolks, lemon zest and vanilla extract. Knead to form a smooth, stiff dough.

4 Put the mixture into the prepared tin and smooth the surface. Bake for about 45 minutes, until firm to the touch. Turn out on to a wire rack and leave to cool.

5 Cut into thin slices, to accompany coffee.

MAKES 10-12

300g (10½oz) plain white or '00' Italian flour
115g (4oz) medium cornmeal
225g (8oz) unsalted butter
200g (7oz) blanched almonds, chopped
200g (7oz) caster sugar
2 egg yolks
finely grated zest of 1 unwaxed lemon
a few drops of pure vanilla extract

Almond and cherry cookies

These bring back warm childhood memories to me and, with their lovely, crumbly texture, are popular with all children.

MAKES 15

115g (4oz) unsalted butter
55g (2oz) caster sugar
a few drops of pure vanilla extract
175g (6oz) self-raising flour
15 whole blanched almonds
15 natural glacé cherries

1 Preheat the oven to 180°C/350°F/gas mark 4. Grease several baking trays.

2 Melt the butter. Add the sugar and vanilla extract, then the flour, and mix to form a firm dough.

3 Shape the mixture into 15 balls and top each with an almond and a cherry. Arrange on the baking trays, leaving plenty of room between each, as they will spread.

4 Bake for 10-15 minutes, until golden. Transfer to a wire rack and leave to cool.

Sardinian macaroons

This recipe was given to me by my Umbrian friend Antoinette, who has a fabulous pastry shop. (Her parents come from Sardinia, where wonderful almonds are grown, thus the Sicilian origin of the recipe.) Use fresh almonds for the best results.

MAKES 25-30

2 egg whites
175g (6oz) caster sugar
175g (6oz) flaked almonds
1 tsp lemon juice

1 Preheat the oven to 170°C/325°F/gas mark 3. Cover several large baking trays with baking parchment.

2 Beat the egg whites until stiff. Fold in the sugar, almonds and lemon juice. Place heaped teaspoons of the mixture, well apart, on the baking trays.

3 Bake for about 20 minutes, until lightly coloured. Leave to cool. Store in an air-tight container.

All Souls' biscuits

These biscuits are brittle and dry like old bones, which is how they got their rather macabre Italian name *ossa dei morti*, meaning 'bones of the dead'. They are eaten all over Italy on 2nd November to celebrate All Souls' Day.

1 Preheat the oven to 180°C/350°F/gas mark 4. Line several baking trays with baking parchment.

2 Roughly chop the almonds and chocolate. Whisk the egg whites until stiff, then gradually add half the sugar until well mixed and the mixture is shiny and stiff. Sprinkle in the remaining sugar. Add the semolina flour, chopped almonds and chocolate, and fold in well.

3 Using 2 teaspoons, shape small portions of the mixture, on the baking trays, into bone-shaped biscuits about 7.5 x 4cm (3 x 1½in). Space the biscuits well apart to allow for spreading.

4 Bake for 30 minutes, until fairly dry but still pale. Cool on a wire rack.

5 For the topping, cut the chocolate and butter into pieces, and melt together in a bowl over a pan of simmering water. Dip the bones into the chocolate, and spread over evenly. Place on a wire rack, and leave to set before serving.

MAKES 18-20

175g (6oz) blanched almonds
175g (6oz) dark chocolate with 70% cocoa solids
2 egg whites
115g (4oz) icing sugar
175g (6oz) semolina flour

topping
175g (6oz) dark chocolate with 70% cocoa solids
25g (1oz) unsalted butter

Apricot almond shortcake

This is the best shortcake recipe I know. It really melts in the mouth. It's a great treat for all the family.

1   To make the shortcake, put the butter and sugar in a large bowl and beat until light and creamy. Add the egg and beat well. Stir in the self-raising and plain flours. Turn out on to a lightly floured surface and knead lightly until smooth. Wrap in greaseproof paper and chill in the fridge for 30 minutes.

2   Meanwhile, make the filling. Put the butter, sugar, egg yolk and vanilla extract in a small bowl and beat until light and fluffy. Stir in the ground almonds and flour. Put the apricots in a food processor or blender, and blend until smooth. Gently fold into the almond mixture.

3   Preheat the oven to 170°C/325°F/gas mark 3. Grease and line a deep 20cm (8in) loose-bottomed cake tin.

4   Divide the dough in half. On a lightly floured surface, roll out each half to a 20cm (8in) round. Place one round into the prepared tin. Spread the filling mixture over the dough, to within 1cm (½in) of the edge. Place the second round of dough over the apricot mixture and press the edges together.

5   Brush with water, then bake for 30-35 minutes until pale golden brown. Leave to stand for 15 minutes before turning out on to a wire rack to cool. Remove the paper lining carefully and place on a baking tray. Turn the oven temperature up to 200°C/400°F/gas mark 6.

6   To make the topping, put the ground almonds and sugar in a bowl. In a small bowl, mix the egg yolks and Amaretto, then gradually stir into the almond mixture. Remove a quarter of the mixture and add 2 tbsp of egg whites. Mix well and use to spread over the sides of the shortcake.

7   Whisk the remaining egg whites until stiff and fold into the reserved almond mixture. Spoon into a piping bag, fitted with a large star nozzle. Pipe zigzag lines in a pattern over the top of the shortcake and pipe small rosettes around the edge. Bake for 8-10 minutes, until the top is lightly browned.

8   Meanwhile, heat the apricot conserve until melted, then sieve into a bowl. Spoon two-thirds of the conserve between the zigzag lines and leave to cool for 10 minutes. Spread the sides with the remaining apricot conserve and coat with the toasted almonds. Leave to cool before serving.

MAKES 8-10

115g (4oz) unsalted butter, softened
115g (4oz) caster sugar
1 egg
100g (3½oz) self-raising flour
100g (3½oz) plain white or '00' Italian flour, plus extra for dusting

filling
40g (1½oz) unsalted butter
2 tbsp caster sugar
1 egg yolk
2-3 dashes of pure vanilla extract
25g (1oz) ground almonds
2 tbsp white flour or '00' Italian flour
225g (8oz) fresh apricots

topping
115g (4oz) ground almonds
3 tbsp caster sugar
6 egg yolks
1 tbsp Amaretto
2 egg whites
115g (4oz) apricot conserve
55g (1oz) flaked almonds, toasted

Juliet kisses

These biscuits are light and delectable. Do make sure that you are precise with the measurements.

MAKES 24

125g (4½oz) unsalted butter, softened
140g (5oz) caster sugar
pinch of salt
2 tsp pure vanilla extract
175g (6oz) plain white or '00' Italian flour
140g (5oz) shelled hazelnuts, ground
1 tbsp cocoa powder
175g (6oz) plain chocolate with 70% cocoa solids

1 Preheat the oven to 180°C/350°F/gas mark 4, and grease a baking sheet.

2 In a bowl, beat together the butter and sugar, then add the salt and vanilla, and mix until smooth. Add the flour and ground nuts, and mix just until blended.

3 Divide the dough into 2 equal parts and add the cocoa to 1 part. Put both doughs on a plate, cover with clingfilm, and chill in the fridge for 1 hour.

4 After an hour's resting, shape the biscuits by rolling small pieces of dough into balls about the size of a chestnut. You should have 24 of each colour. Place on the prepared baking sheet. Bake the cookies for about 15 minutes, until firm. Leave to cool on a wire rack.

5 Break the chocolate into pieces and melt in a bowl over simmering water. When the biscuits are cooked and tepid, sandwich the pale and dark biscuits together with melted chocolate.

Chocolate cherry biscuits

Italians indulge in these biscuits as a treat after Lent. Of course, you can enjoy them at any time of the year.

1 Sift the flour and baking powder into a large bowl. Dice and rub in the butter until the mixture is coarse. Add the eggs and sugar, and mix with your hands until a ball of dough is formed. On a lightly floured surface, knead the dough until smooth. Wrap in greaseproof paper and chill in the fridge for an hour.

2 Preheat the oven to 180°C/350°F/gas mark 4. Lightly grease several baking trays.

3 On a lightly floured surface, use a rolling pin to flatten the dough. Sprinkle the chopped nuts over the surface and knead them into the dough with your hands.

4 Divide the dough in half. Roll out one-half into a 30cm (12in) square. Trim the edges so that they are straight. With a fluted pastry wheel, cut the dough into 4 rows one way, and 6 rows the other way, to make 24 biscuits. Repeat with the remaining dough, to make 48 biscuits in total. Place the biscuits well apart on the baking trays.

5 Bake for 10-15 minutes, until lightly browned. Transfer to a wire rack and leave to cool.

6 When cold, spread the jam on half the biscuits and sandwich them together in pairs.

7 Melt the chocolate and, using a small spoon, spread a little of the chocolate evenly over the top of each biscuit. Place on a wire rack and leave to dry completely before serving.

MAKES 24

350g (12oz) plain white or '00' Italian flour, plus extra for dusting
½ tsp baking powder
115g (4oz) unsalted butter, softened
2 eggs, lightly beaten
85g (3oz) caster sugar
40g (1½oz) blanched almonds, finely chopped
2-3 tbsp cherry conserve
115g (4oz) dark chocolate with 70% cocoa solids

Honey and spice twists

These are traditionally eaten on Christmas Eve – a huge pyramid of golden, light pastries, smothered in honey and mixed spice. My grandmother used to get up early on Christmas Eve especially to make them. They are delicious, but take a bit of practice to make perfect.

SERVES 4-5

15g (½oz) fresh yeast, or 1½ tsp dried yeast
   and pinch of caster sugar
150ml (5fl oz) warm water
225g (8oz) plain white or '00' Italian flour
pinch of salt
1 egg, beaten
olive oil, for deep-frying

to serve
caster sugar, for dusting
2 tsp ground mixed spice
3 tbsp honey

1 Blend the fresh yeast with 2 tbsp of the hand-hot water. If using dried yeast, sprinkle it into 2 tbsp of the water with the sugar. Leave in a warm place for 15 minutes, until frothy.

2 Sift the flour and salt into a large bowl and make a well in the centre. Pour the yeast liquid, beaten egg and some of the remaining water into the centre and mix together, gradually adding the remaining water, to form a dough.

3 On a well-floured surface, knead the dough for 10 minutes, until smooth. Put the dough in a lightly oiled bowl, cover with a clean tea-towel and leave to rest for 20 minutes.

4 Take a large chestnut-sized piece of dough and roll into a thin sausage-shape, then cross the ends over to form a loop at one end. Continue with the dough to make 15 twists.

5 Heat the olive oil in a saucepan until very lightly smoking. Cook 5 pieces of dough at a time. When they bob to the surface, drain on kitchen paper.

6 When all the dough is cooked, dust the twists with caster sugar and the mixed spice. Pile them into a pyramid on a serving plate.

7 Heat the honey in a small saucepan, then pour over the top of the twists. Serve on the day that you make them.

Italian lady's fingers

As the Italian name *savoiardi* suggests, these biscuits come from Savoy, which is north-west of Turin in the Piedmont region of Italy. Savoiardi are used in a range of desserts. In Italy, they are given to children as a snack. Make up a batch and store in an air-tight tin so that they are always available.

MAKES 12

3 eggs, separated
1 tsp pure vanilla extract
85g (3oz) self-raising flour
1 tsp baking powder
¼ tsp salt
85g (3oz) caster sugar

1 Preheat the oven to 180°C/350°F/gas mark 4.

2 Beat the egg yolks until thick, then beat in the vanilla extract. In a bowl, sift the flour and baking powder together.

3 Whisk the egg whites until stiff, then whisk in the salt and sugar until the whites are glossy and very stiff. Using a metal spoon, fold the egg yolks into the egg whites, followed by the sifted flour.

4 Drop tbsp of the batter on to an ungreased baking tray, and spread to form fingers measuring about 20 x 6cm (8 x 2½in).

5 Bake for 10 minutes, until golden. Transfer to a wire rack and leave to cool.

Cornmeal biscuits

These are delicious, crisp Tuscan biscuits. Serve them with coffee for breakfast, as we do in Italy.

1 Melt the butter. Put the flour, polenta and sugar into a large bowl and pour in the egg, milk, melted butter and vanilla extract. Mix well. Turn out on to a lightly floured surface and knead the dough. Wrap in greaseproof paper and chill in the fridge for 30 minutes.

2 Preheat the oven to 180°C/350°F/gas mark 4. Grease several baking trays.

3 On a lightly floured surface, roll out the dough to 2cm (¾in) thick and, using a 6cm (2½in) fluted or plain cutter, cut into rounds. Place on the prepared baking trays.

4 Bake for 15 minutes, until crisp and yellow. Transfer to a wire rack and leave to cool. Store in an air-tight jar.

5 If wished, serve dusted with sifted icing sugar.

MAKES 28

115g (4oz) unsalted butter
200g (7oz) plain white or '00' Italian flour
300g (10½oz) fine polenta
115g (4oz) caster sugar
3 eggs, beaten
100ml (3½fl oz) milk
1 tsp pure vanilla extract
icing sugar, for dusting (optional)

Twice-baked cookies

Baking twice makes these cookies dry and ideal for dipping into *Vin Santo* at the end of a meal. There are many variations of these cookies – for instance, you may want to experiment using hazelnuts instead of almonds.

MAKES 24

280g (10oz) plain white or '00' Italian
  flour
140g (5oz) caster sugar
1 tsp baking powder
2 eggs
1 egg yolk
1 tbsp vanilla extract
115g (4oz) whole blanched almonds

1 Preheat the oven to 180°C/350°F/gas mark 4. Grease a baking tray.

2 Put the flour, sugar, baking powder, eggs, egg yolk and vanilla extract into a bowl and mix well together by hand.

3 Add the almonds and knead until mixed together. Divide the dough into 6 pieces, then form each piece into a roll and flatten into a flat cigar shape. Arrange on the prepared baking tray. Bake for 20 minutes.

4 Cut each biscuit into 4 pieces, then bake for a further 10 minutes, until golden. Transfer to a wire rack and leave to cool.

Sweet pastry beans

These biscuits are shaped like broad beans. They are traditionally made for All Saints' Day on 1 November.

1 Preheat the oven to 180°C/350°F/Gas mark 4. Grease several baking trays and dust with flour.

2 Put the sugar and almonds in a food processor and blend until finely ground.

3 Put the flour and cinnamon in a bowl and dice and rub in the butter. Add the almonds and sugar, egg and lemon zest, and mix together until the mixture is firm and smooth.

4 Roll the dough into a thin, long cylinder, then divide into pieces the size of a walnut. Shape each piece to resemble a broad bean.

5 Place on the baking trays and bake for 15 minutes, until light golden in colour. Transfer to a wire rack to cool and crisp. If liked, dust with sifted icing sugar before serving.

MAKES 30

115g (4oz) caster sugar
115g (4oz) whole blanched almonds
175g (6oz) plain white or '00' Italian flour
1 tsp ground cinnamon
15g (½oz) unsalted butter, chilled
1 egg, beaten
finely grated zest of 1 unwaxed lemon
icing sugar, for dusting (optional)

Venetian liqueur biscuits

These little biscuits are good in May from the local *pasticceria*. They can be flavoured with any liqueur – Limoncello and cherry liqueur are very good.

MAKES 12

5 eggs, separated
135g (4½oz) caster sugar
140g (5oz) plain white or '00' Italian flour
pinch of salt
1 tbsp Maraschino, Limoncello or even Cointreau
icing sugar, for dusting

1 Preheat the oven to 180°C/350°F/gas mark 4. Line a baking tray with baking parchment.

2 Beat the egg yolks and sugar together in a bowl until white and creamy. Sift in the flour and salt, and fold in gently.

3 Beat the egg whites until stiff and fold into the mixture with the liqueur of your choice.

4 Place the mixture carefully in a piping bag. Pipe lengths of about 7.5cm (3in) on to the lined baking tray, then bake for 6 minutes, until nicely brown.

5 Leave to cool on a wire rack and dust with icing sugar.

Venetian biscuits

These biscuits used to be given to children by their godparents on Confirmation Day. They are served with fruit and coffee, and dipped by my family in the last of the wine.

MAKES 24

225g (8oz) plain white or '00' Italian flour
225g (8oz) caster sugar
4 egg yolks
1 egg
knob of unsalted butter
pinch of salt

1 Preheat the oven to 180°C/350°F/gas mark 4. Grease a baking sheet.

2 Beat everything together to form a dough.

3 Roll out on a lightly floured surface and cut into strips about the size of your finger. Form these into 'S' shapes or rings and place on the greased baking sheet.

4 Bake for about 15 minutes, until brown. Allow to cool on a wire rack.

Pastry bows

These little pastries are popular with coffee throughout Italy. I got the recipe from Rosalba, a friend from Minori (where my family come from). They are made in Minori for the Carnival of Santa Trofimiane, the patron saint of the village. Everything is weighed depending on the weight of the eggs in their shells.

1 Beat the eggs until light and full of volume. Mix in the sugar, butter, *grappa* and salt. Begin to add the flour slowly, mixing until you have a firm dough.

2 Roll the dough out thinly on a floured surface and cut into oblong shapes of 7.5cm (3in) long. Tie the dough in bows – this I can remember my grandmother doing. Or you could simply cut 2 diagonal slashes in each piece of pastry so they will puff up during cooking.

3 Deep-fry in very hot oil for 5-6 minutes, or until golden. Drain on kitchen paper and serve hot with a dusting of icing sugar. They are equally good served cold.

MAKES 24

6 eggs, weighed in their shells
½ the egg weight in caster sugar
½ the egg weight in unsalted butter, softened
2 tbsp grappa
generous pinch of salt
½ the egg weight in plain white or '00' Italian flour
sunflower or groundnut oil, for deep-frying
icing sugar, for dusting

Sweets

The Italians have as sweet a tooth as anyone in Europe. They particularly love chocolate in cakes, puddings, biscuits and indeed sweets. Some Italian sweets, such as truffles, will be familiar. Others, such as stuffed figs and prunes coated or drizzled with chocolate, will be rather less well known, but are still characteristically Italian. Dried fruits and nuts are used in sweets such as nougat. In my home region of Calabria there is a major production of *frutta candita*, or candied fruit, because so much citrus fruit is grown in the hot south. These *candite*, a recipe for which I give here, are used in many sweets, cakes and puddings, particularly *panettone*, *panforte*, *cassata* and *cannoli*.

Chocolate salami

This is a rather special chocolate and biscuit mixture, in the shape of a salami. It is easy to make, and goes beautifully with coffee at the end of a meal. Take it as a gift when you go to eat with friends, and everyone will enjoy it.

SERVES 6-8

55g (2oz) split blanched almonds
20 *petit beurre* biscuits
225g (8oz) dark chocolate with 70% cocoa solids
175g (6oz) unsalted butter
3 tbsp brandy
25g (1oz) ground almonds
1 tbsp cocoa powder, for dusting

1 Spread the blanched almonds evenly in a grill pan and grill for 2-3 minutes, shaking the pan frequently until the nuts are golden. Finely grind the nuts in a food processor. Transfer to a bowl.

2 Chop the biscuits in the food processor until roughly crushed. Set aside 3 tbsp, and put the rest in a second bowl.

3 Break the chocolate into pieces and put in a small saucepan. Cut the butter into small pieces, add to the chocolate with the brandy, and heat gently until melted. Pour the melted chocolate mixture into the bowl of crushed biscuits, add the nuts, and mix together well.

4 Leave the mixture in the fridge for about 2 hours (or, if time is short, in the freezer for 30 minutes), until it is solid.

5 Sprinkle the reserved biscuit crumbs on to a piece of baking parchment and turn the chocolate mixture on to it. With a palette knife and your hands, shape into a sausage about 23cm (9in) long and roll in the biscuit crumbs.

6 Put the roll back in the fridge until ready to serve, sprinkled with sifted cocoa powder and cut up into slices as thick or thin as you wish.

Chocolate truffles

These are the most scrumptious, wickedly rich truffles, and they really do make the perfect gift at any time of the year. Wrap them in clear Cellophane, or splash out on a small gift box for them, and you have a present anyone will welcome.

SERVES 12

55g (2oz) *petit beurre* biscuits
85g (3oz) dark chocolate with 70% cocoa solids
25g (1oz) shelled hazelnuts, finely chopped
35g (1¼oz) raisins
1 tbsp rum
cocoa powder, for dusting

1 Put the biscuits in a polythene bag and crush with a rolling pin.

2 Break the chocolate into a heat-proof bowl over a pan of simmering water and heat until melted. Remove from the heat and mix with the biscuit crumbs. Add the remaining ingredients, except for the cocoa powder, and mix together. Leave to cool for 1 hour.

3 Form the mixture into small balls the size of a cherry, and dust with cocoa powder. Place in little sweet papers, and store in a cool, dry place.

Almond stuffed figs in chocolate

This is a delicacy from Calabria, a southern region of Italy. Figs are plentiful in Italy and this is a wonderful way of using them. They are so good to make for a gift – perhaps even more so in countries where figs are less common.

1 Spread the almonds on a sheet of foil under the grill, and toast until golden, turning them frequently.

2 Slit the figs and place an almond inside each. Roll the figs in the orange zest.

3 Break the chocolate into a heat-proof bowl standing over a saucepan of simmering water, and heat until melted.

4 Using a fork, dip the figs in the chocolate, then place them on baking parchment and leave to dry.

SERVES 12

12 whole blanched almonds
12 dried figs, preferable Italian
very finely grated zest of 3 unwaxed
  oranges
225g (8oz) dark chocolate with 70%
  cocoa solids

Boozy stuffed prunes drizzled with chocolate

Prunes are so often neglected, so I am continuing my quest for them to be taken more seriously as a delicious fruit. Pruneaux d'Agen from France are my favourites. Serve these with ice-cream as a dessert, or with coffee.

SERVES 6

18 prunes, preferably unsulphured
300ml (10fl oz) dessert wine
55g (2oz) blanched almonds
finely grated zest of 2 unwaxed oranges
115g (4oz) mascarpone
55g (2oz) plain chocolate with 70% cocoa solids
55g (2oz) white chocolate
icing sugar, to dust

1 Put the prunes in a bowl, pour over the wine and leave to soak overnight.

2 The next day, toast the almonds on a sheet of foil under the grill, turning them frequently. Leave to cool, then finely chop.

3 Drain the prunes and dry with kitchen paper, then remove the stones. Put the orange zest, mascarpone and almonds into a bowl and mix together. Use the mixture to stuff the prunes.

4 Break the plain chocolate into a heat-proof bowl, place over a saucepan of simmering water and heat until melted.

5 Using a fork, dip the prunes in the plain chocolate, then place on baking parchment and leave to dry.

6 Melt the white chocolate in a separate bowl in the same way as you did the plain chocolate. Fill a piping bag, fitted with a small plain nozzle, with the melted white chocolate and pipe lines on the prunes. Alternatively, using a teaspoon, drizzle the melted white chocolate over the prunes. Leave to dry.

7 To serve, arrange 3 prunes on each plate and dust with sifted icing sugar.

Honey, nut and fruit nougat

A speciality from Siena, this flat cake, or 'strong bread', has a nougat-like texture, and it is rich in candied peel, toasted nuts and spices. It has become traditional at Christmas.

1 Preheat the oven to 150°C/300°F/gas mark 2. Line with baking paper a 20cm (8in) flan tin.

2 Toast the hazelnuts and almonds on a sheet of foil under the grill until golden, turning them frequently. Roughly chop and leave to cool. Finely chop the candied peel.

3 Put the nuts, candied peel, cocoa powder, flour, cinnamon and mixed spice in a bowl and mix well together.

4 Put the sugar and honey in a saucepan and heat gently until a sugar thermometer registers 115°C/240°F, or until a little of the mixture, dropped into a cup of water, forms a ball. Immediately remove from the heat, add to the nut mixture and, working quickly, mix well.

5 Turn into the prepared tin and, using a tablespoon dipped in hot water, spread the mixture flat, making sure that it is no more than 1cm (½in) thick.

6 Bake for 30 minutes. Leave to cool in the tin, then turn out on to a wire rack and peel off the paper.

7 Sprinkle the top thickly with sifted icing sugar and cinnamon, and serve cut into small wedges.

SERVES 8-10

85g (3oz) shelled hazelnuts
85g (3oz) blanched almonds
175g (6oz) candied peel
25g (1oz) cocoa powder
55g (2oz) plain white or '00' Italian flour
½ tsp ground cinnamon
¼ tsp ground mixed spice
115g (4oz) caster sugar
115g (4oz) honey

to finish
2 tbsp icing sugar
1 tsp ground cinnamon

Sesame and almond nougat

This recipe demonstrates the extensive use of honey and almonds in Italian cooking. Sesame seeds are full of calcium, and almonds are good for you too, so don't feel guilty about enjoying this recipe!

1 Brush a baking tray and rolling pin generously with almond oil.

2 Put the honey in a saucepan and heat gently until melted. Add the sugar and slowly bring to the boil. Add the sesame seeds and almonds, and heat, stirring all the time, until the mixture thickens.

3 Pour on to the greased baking tray and flatten with the rolling pin into a square of about 28cm (11in) and 5mm (¼in) thick. Leave to cool slightly.

4 Using a sharp knife, cut into small 4cm (1½in) squares. Leave to cool completely. Store in an air-tight tin.

MAKES ABOUT 48 SQUARES

almond oil, for greasing
200g (7oz) fragrant honey
55g (2oz) caster sugar
225g (8oz) sesame seeds
200g (7oz) blanched almonds, toasted and roughly chopped

Candied orange and lemon peel

This is a speciality from southern Italy, where many oranges and lemons are grown. This is one way of using their skins in cooking. Consequently, candied zest appears in many southern Italian recipes.

MAKES ABOUT 55-85G (2-3OZ)

280g (10oz) granulated sugar
2 smooth-skinned unwaxed oranges or
  lemons
caster sugar, for sprinkling

1 To make the syrup, put the granulated sugar and 600ml (1 pint) water in a saucepan and heat until dissolved. Boil for 90 seconds.

2 Wash and dry the orange or lemons. Using a swivel-blade vegetable peeler, peel the zest into strips, then chop into matchsticks or other shapes.

3 Add the zest to the syrup and boil for 5 minutes if matchsticks, 10 minutes if larger. Using a slotted spoon, lift them out of the syrup and cool on wire racks. (You can use the syrup again.)

4 Sprinkle with caster sugar and roll the zest in this until well coated. Shake off any excess sugar and store the zest in an air-tight box

Dried figs stuffed with ricotta and almonds

This is a classical Christmas treat. Stuffed figs have been around since ancient times – the ingredients used here were staples of shepherds living in central Italy before Rome was founded.

SERVES 4-6

18 large dried figs, preferably Italian
175g (6oz) fresh ricotta
18 blanched whole almonds, toasted

1 Using a paring knife, slit a pocket in the figs, cutting from the base towards the stem.

2 Spoon about 2 tsp ricotta into each slit. Slip an almond in on top.

3 Gently pinch the figs closed with your fingers, then place in a serving dish.

Violette
candite
€ 10,50
l'etto

Breads

Bread is one of the major strands of Italian cooking and eating, and throughout the country there is a huge variety of this everyday food. Sweet breads, though, are more of a regional and special occasion treat. *Panettone*, the Christmas bread of Milan, needs virtually no introduction, as we have all seen the ribboned boxes suspended from the ceilings of Italian delis as the festive season approaches. The Easter *pandolce* is even richer in its content of dried fruit and nuts. In fact, many breads are made for Easter, usually in the shape of a ring large or small (*ciambellone* and *ciambellina* respectively), and either sweet or savoury. A fruit loaf, or rolls, is made with grapes in the north of Italy for Easter, and another Easter bread, not included here, is made in the shape of a dove.

Panettone

Panettone comes from Milan in northern Italy. The breads are exported in attractive tall boxes, which can be seen hanging in Italian delicatessens all over the world. *Panettone* made at home is not so tall as the commercial varieties, and its texture is not quite so open, but it makes a deliciously light alternative to heavy Christmas cakes.

1 Grease the insides of 3 clean 400g tomato tin cans or similar. Cut 3 strips of baking parchment, each measuring 55 x 33cm (22 x 12in). Fold each piece in half lengthways, then use to line the tins. Line the bases with a circle of baking parchment.

2 Blend the fresh yeast with 2 tbsp of milk until smooth, then stir in the remaining milk. If using dried yeast, sprinkle it into the milk and leave in a warm place for 15 minutes until frothy.

3 Sift the flour into a large bowl and make a well in the centre. Pour the yeast liquid into the well and, using a wooden spoon, gradually draw in the flour from the sides of the bowl until well mixed. Knead on a lightly floured work surface for 10 minutes until smooth. Form into a ball and place in a lightly oiled bowl. Cover with a clean tea-towel and leave to use in a warm place for 45 minutes, or until doubled in size.

4 Knead the softened butter into the dough with 2 of the egg yolks, the sugar, candied peel, sultanas and nutmeg. Cover and leave to stand, again in a warm place, for a further 45 minutes, or until doubled in size.

5 Divide the dough into 3 pieces and knead each piece for 2-3 minutes. Form each piece into a smooth ball and place inside the cans. Leave in a warm place for about 30 minutes, or until risen to the top of the cans.

6 Meanwhile, preheat the oven to 200°C/400°F/gas mark 6. Brush the remaining egg yolk over the dough. Bake for 20 minutes, then lower the temperature to 180°C/350°F/gas mark 4 and bake for a further 20 minutes, or until a skewer inserted in the centre comes out clean. Leave to cool in the cans.

7 The *panettone* can be stored in an air-tight tin for up to a week.

SERVES 9, FROM 3 SMALL PANETTONE

4 tsp fresh yeast or 2¼ tsp dried yeast
225ml (8fl oz) hand-hot milk
350g (12oz) plain white or Italian '00' flour
100g (3½oz) unsalted butter, softened
3 egg yolks
50g (1¾oz) caster sugar
85g (3oz) chopped candied peel
50g (1¾oz) sultanas
1½ tsp grated nutmeg
icing sugar, for dusting

Ring-shaped Easter bread with nut brittle

Coming after Lent, and all its associated abstinence, this is a true celebration bread. We would take this bread on our Easter Monday picnic.

MAKES 1 LOAF

2 tsp dried yeast
100ml (3½fl oz) hand-hot milk
600g (1¼lb) strong white flour
2 tsp salt
115g (4oz) granulated sugar
finely grated zest of 3 unwaxed lemons
115g (4oz) unsalted butter, softened
3 eggs, beaten
100ml (3½fl oz) water

topping
4 tsp ground cinnamon
3 tbsp granulated sugar
115g (4oz) blanched almonds, toasted and
   roughly chopped
1 egg yolk

1 Sprinkle the yeast into the milk in a small bowl. Leave for 5 minutes, and stir to dissolve.

2 Mix the flour, salt, sugar and lemon zest together in a large bowl. Make a well in the centre of the mixture, then add to it the butter, eggs and the yeasted milk. Mix in the flour from the sides of the well. Add the water, 1 tbsp at a time, as needed, to form a soft, sticky dough.

3 Turn the dough out on to a lightly floured work surface. Knead for about 10 minutes, until smooth, springy and elastic.

4 Put the dough in a clean, oiled bowl and cover with a clean tea-towel. Leave to rise for about 4 hours, until doubled in size.

5 Knock back the dough, then leave to rest, covered with a tea-towel, for about 10 minutes. Grease a baking sheet.

6 Divide the dough into 2 equal pieces and roll each piece into a 40cm (16in) long rope. Twist the 2 dough ropes together. Place the shaped dough rope on the prepared baking sheet. Shape it into a ring by bringing the two ends of the rope together. Pinch them to seal, and cover with a tea-towel. Leave for about 1½ hours, until doubled in size.

7 Preheat the oven to 200°C/400°F/gas mark 6.

8 To make the topping, mix the cinnamon, sugar, almonds and egg yolk together in a bowl. Use a rubber spatula to spread the mixture evenly over the top of the ring.

9 Bake for 45 minutes, until golden and hollow-sounding when tapped underneath. Turn the loaf out on to a wire rack and leave to cool.

Rosemary raisin bread

Tuscany is famous for its rosemary, which is characteristically strong and aromatic. This Florentine bread, made with local herb and dried grapes, is delicious with a mild goat's cheese.

1 Sprinkle the yeast into the water in a bowl. Leave for 5 minutes, and stir to dissolve the yeast.

2 Mix the flour, salt and milk powder in a large bowl and make a well in the centre. Add the yeast liquid and all the remaining ingredients to the well. Mix the flour into the yeast mixture to form a soft, sticky dough. Add extra flour, 1 tbsp at a time, if the dough is too moist.

3 Turn the dough out on to a lightly floured work surface. Knead for about 10 minutes, until silky, springy and elastic.

4 Put the dough in a clean, oiled bowl and cover with a clean tea-towel. Leave to rise for about 2 hours, or until doubled in size.

5 Knock back and chafe the risen dough for 5 minutes; this means rotating the dough in a circle, while applying a light downwards pressure to the sides, cupping the dough with the inside of your hands. Do this until the dough is smooth and round. Leave to rest for 10 minutes. Oil 2 baking sheets.

6 Divide the dough into 2 equal pieces and shape each into a round loaf. Place on the prepared baking sheets and cover with tea-towels. Leave for about 1 hour, until doubled in size. These loaves will spread and look slightly flat after rising, but they will rise up dramatically during the initial stages of baking.

7 Preheat the oven to 200°C/400°F/gas mark 6.

8 Cut a slash 1cm (½in) deep across the top of each loaf, then another in the opposite direction to make an 'X'.

9 Bake for 45 minutes, until golden brown and hollow-sounding when tapped underneath. Turn out on to a wire rack and leave to cool.

MAKES 2 LOAVES

2 tsp dried yeast
100ml (3½fl oz) hand-hot water
450g (1lb) strong white flour
1½ tsp salt
2 tbsp milk powder
1 tbsp chopped fresh rosemary
225g (8oz) raisins
4 tbsp olive oil
4 eggs, beaten

Orange, apricot and walnut bread

This *pandolce* is another celebratory bread – a 'soft bread' - from my aunt in Minori. It is usually made for Easter.

MAKES 1 LOAF

115g (4oz) dried apricots, preferably
  unsulphured
zest of 1 unwaxed orange
55g (2oz) unsalted butter
10g (¼oz) fresh yeast, or ½ tsp dried yeast
200g (7oz) strong plain flour
75g (2¾oz) caster sugar
55g (2oz) walnut kernels, chopped
2 eggs, beaten

topping
1 tbsp honey
2 tbsp orange juice
25g (1oz) walnut kernels, ground
6 dried apricots, preferably unsulphered,
  chopped

1   Preheat the oven to 180°C/350°F/gas mark 4. Lightly grease and flour a 1.2 litre (2 pint) ring mould.

2   Put the apricots and orange zest in the food processor and blend at a low speed. The fruit must be minced, but not pulpy.

3   Pour into a pan and add the butter. Cook over a low heat, stirring, until the butter is melted, then remove from the heat.

4   Mix the yeast with 2 tbsp hand-hot water. Combine the flour with the yeast liquid, sugar and chopped walnuts. Add the beaten eggs, melted butter and fruit. Mix well. Pour into the prepared mould and level the surface.

5   Bake for 1¼ hours. Remove the cake from the mould and leave to cool.

6   In the meantime, prepare the topping. In a saucepan, bring the honey and orange juice to the boil and let them boil for about 30 seconds, stirring.

7   Put the ground walnuts into a bowl, and mix with half the honey and orange liquid. Put the apricots into the second half of the liquid and warm on a slow heat for 1 minute. Put the walnuts down the middle of the cake and put the apricots on the sides. Leave to cool before serving.

Fresh grape and fennel flatbread

This sweet flatbread, made to celebrate the grape harvest in October, is best served warm as an accompaniment to coffee or as a dessert. *Schiacciata* means 'squashed', as the grapes are squashed on the top. The bread can also be made with raisins soaked in *Vin Santo* inside, and fresh grapes on top.

MAKES 1 LOAF

15g (½oz) fresh yeast or 2 tsp dried yeast
175ml (6fl oz) hand-hot water
55g (2oz) caster sugar, plus 2 tbsp
3 tbsp olive oil, plus extra for greasing
350g (12oz) strong white flour
1 tsp salt
450g (1lb) black grapes, preferably
  seedless
¼-½ tsp fennel seed
1 egg, beaten, for glazing

1 Cream the fresh yeast with the water. If using dry yeast, sprinkle it into the water with a pinch of the sugar, and leave in a warm place for 15 minutes until frothy.

2 Put the flour, salt and the 2 tbsp sugar in a large bowl. Make a well in the centre, add the yeast liquid and the oil, and beat together to form a soft, slightly sticky dough, adding a little more flour if necessary.

3 Turn the dough out on to a floured work surface and knead lightly until just smooth. Put in a clean, oiled bowl, cover with a clean tea-towel and leave in a warm place for about an hour, or until doubled in size. Brush a large, edged baking tray with oil.

4 Meanwhile, halve and, if necessary, remove the seeds from the grapes. Put in a small bowl with the remaining sugar and the fennel seed. Cover and leave to marinate while the dough is rising.

5 On a well-floured work surface, roll out half the dough to an oblong measuring about 28 x 25cm (11 x 10in). Place on the prepared baking tray and top with three-quarters of the grapes, fennel seed and juices, spreading to within 1cm (½in) of the edge of the dough. Roll out the remaining dough, and place over the top of the first oblong, dampening and sealing the edges well. Brush with the beaten egg to glaze, and spoon over the remaining grape mixture. Leave in a warm place for 15-20 minutes, or until doubled in size.

6 Meanwhile, preheat the oven to 200°C/400°F/gas mark 6.

7 Bake for 35-40 minutes, or until well browned. Serve warm, cut into squares.

Crisp bread rings

These bread rings from Puglia are eaten throughout southern Italy as an appetizer to be served with drinks. They are similar to a bagel (which is why they are in the bread chapter), but crunchy. They keep for up to a month in an air-tight tin, and children love them.

1 Blend the fresh yeast with the water. If using dried yeast, sprinkle it into the water with the sugar and leave in a warm place for 15 minutes, until frothy.

2 Put 225g (8oz) of the flour in a large bowl and make a well in the centre. Pour the yeast liquid into the well and, using a wooden spoon, incorporate only half of the flour. Cover the bowl with a clean tea-towel and leave the dough to rise in a warm place for 1 hour, until doubled in size.

3 Put the remaining flour in a mound on a clean work surface and make a well in the centre. Put the yeast mixture in the well with the remaining unincorporated flour. Add the oil, 2 of the eggs, the fennel seed, and 1 tsp each of salt and pepper.

4 Mix together all the ingredients in the well, then start incorporating the flour from the inside edge of the well. Keep mixing until all but about 5 tbsp of the flour is incorporated. Knead for 5 minutes.

5 Cut the dough into 4 pieces. Using the 4 fingers of both hands, lightly roll each piece until 63cm (25in) long. Divide into 5 equal pieces, then take each piece and connect the two ends together to form a circle. Leave to rest for 15 minutes.

6 Meanwhile, preheat the oven to 200°C/400°F/gas mark 6. Lightly oil 2 baking trays.

7 Fill a large saucepan or flame-proof casserole with water and bring to the boil. When boiling, add some salt and then put in 4 or 5 dough rings and boil for 30 seconds. Remove with a slotted spoon, and allow to drain well. Continue until all the rings have been boiled.

8 Put all the rings on the prepared baking trays, brush with the remaining beaten egg and bake for 30 minutes, until golden brown. Transfer to a wire rack and leave to cool.

MAKES 20

25g (1oz) fresh yeast, or 1 tbsp dried yeast
    and 1 tsp caster sugar
150ml (5fl oz) hand-hot water
800g (1¾lb) strong white flour
2 tbsp extra virgin olive oil
3 eggs, beaten
2 tsp fennel seed
salt and pepper

Pandolce with saffron

This Easter bread is bright yellow in colour, and rich in flavour. It is great for breakfast and lovely toasted if there is any left over.

1 Soak the saffron in 1 tbsp hot water for an hour, then strain the liquid and keep aside.

2 Crumble the yeast into the milk, and leave until a little bubbly round the edges.

3 Put the flour into a large bowl with the salt. Rub in the softened butter to form a breadcrumb consistency. Add the sugar, grated lemon zest, the saffron with its liquid and the yeast melted in the milk. Mix together with the raisins and candied peel until you have a smooth paste. Grease a baking sheet.

4 Shape the dough into a circle, and lay on a greased baking sheet. Cover with a thick, clean tea-towel, and let the dough rise in a warm place for 1½ hours, or until doubled in size.

5 Preheat the oven to 180°C/350°F/gas mark 4.

6 Bake the loaf for 1 hour.

7 Remove the bread from the tin, and while still warm, paint with honey. Leave to cool on a wire rack.

8 Serve in thin wedges.

SERVES 6

1 tsp saffron strands
15g (½oz) fresh yeast
150ml (5fl oz) hand-hot milk
450g (1lb) strong flour
1 tsp salt
85g (3oz) unsalted butter, softened
25g (1oz) caster sugar
1 tbsp grated lemon zest (from an unwaxed lemon)
175g (6oz) raisins
25g (1oz) candied orange peel, cut into small cubes
2 tbsp honey

Walnut bread

This is a special cake-bread to celebrate the autumn walnut season. I love to eat it with strong black coffee. My sister has two magnificent walnut trees in her English garden.

MAKES 1 LOAF

200g (7oz) shelled walnuts, preferably
  fresh
25g (1oz) unsalted butter, softened
1 tbsp walnut oil
200g (7oz) caster sugar
1 egg, beaten
2 tsp pure vanilla extract
275g (9½oz) plain flour
generous pinch of salt
1 tsp baking powder
250ml (9fl oz) milk

1 Preheat the oven to 180°C/350°F/gas mark 4. Grease and base line with baking parchment a 450g (1lb) loaf tin.

2 Roast the walnuts in a roasting tin for 8 minutes. Leave them to cool, then coarsely chop them.

3 Cream the butter, oil and sugar together in a mixing bowl, then work in the egg. Beat the mixture thoroughly. Add the nuts and vanilla extract.

4 Sift the flour, salt and baking powder into the bowl, add the milk, and stir well to make a sloppy batter.

5 Pour the batter into the prepared tin and bake for 40 minutes. Turn out on to a wire rack and cool.

6 Serve in thin slices with coffee, or it's surprisingly delicious with cheese.

Pine kernel bread

This is a southern Italian breakfast bread. In Sardinia they usually make this bread with almonds.

1 Soak the zests and sultanas in some water for 2 hours, until the sultanas are plump.

2 Put the tepid water in a bowl, crumble over the yeast, and mix until you have a smooth liquid.

3 Mix the salt and flour together in a large bowl. Rub in the butter until the mixture resembles breadcrumbs. Make a well in the centre and pour in the egg, sultana mixture and yeast mixture. Mix the yeast, egg and sultanas together in the well, then gradually work in the flour to make a very soft dough.

4 Turn the dough out on to a floured work surface. Knead for 5 minutes. Place the dough in an oiled bowl, cover with clingfilm, and leave to rise in a warm place for 3 hours.

5 Grease a baking sheet.

6 Turn the risen dough out on to a floured work surface. Sprinkle with the hazelnuts and pine kernels and gently work them in. When they are evenly distributed, shape the dough into a ball, then pat it into a round about 20cm (8in) in diameter and 4cm (1½in) thick. Place the dough on the prepared baking sheet. Slip the sheet into a large plastic bag. Seal and let the dough rise for a further hour.

7 Preheat the oven to 200°C/400°F/gas mark 6.

8 Uncover the dough and bake for about 35 minutes. Transfer to a wire rack. Dust with icing sugar.

MAKES 1 LOAF

finely grated zest and juice of 2
   unwaxed oranges
finely grated zest of 1 unwaxed
   lemon
100g (3½oz) sultanas
2 tbsp water at body temperature
15g (½oz) fresh yeast
2 tsp sea salt
400g (14oz) strong white bread flour
150g (5½oz) unsalted butter, diced
1 egg, beaten
40g (1½oz) shelled hazelnuts, toasted
75g (2¾oz) pine kernels, toasted
icing sugar, for dusting

Index

Acknowledgements

Thanks are due to the following:

• Richard, my husband, for his quiet gentle ways and his yummy food. Thank you, darling.
• Susan Fleming, my editor, for her strong professional approach, her energy and dedication. A wonderfully good person, full of life and fun. An enormous thank you yet again.
• Rebecca Spry, my commissioning editor, for her tireless hard work and determination. A great mind.
• Francesca Yorke, for stunning work. A joy to work with, and thank you yet again.
• Pippa Cuthbert, a name to look out for. Pippa styled all the food and was the home economist. We have worked together for many years, and she is a true pro.
• Miranda Harvey, for her huge talent and dedication, she does beautiful work.
• Yasia Williams-Leedham, for her enthusiasm and keenness. Thank you so much for all you do.
• Nessy Cumberledge, my very great friend, who did the typing under incredible pressure, and did a great job.
• Rosie and Eric Treuille, for providing a great source of inspiration to us all at *Books for Cooks*.